heartwarmers of love

Award-winning Stories of Love, Romance, Friends, and Family

BY
AZRIELA JAFFE

Adams Media Corporation
Holbrook, Massachusetts

Published by
Adams Media Corporation
260 Center Street, Holbrook, MA 02343. U.S.A.
www.adamsmedia.com

ISBN: 1-58062-471-5

Printed in Canada.

J I H G F E D C B A

Heartwarmers of love : award winning stories of love, romance, friends, and family /
[compiled by] Azriela Jaffe.
p.   cm.
ISBN 1-58062-471-5
1. Conduct of life. I. Jaffe, Azriela.
BJ1597.H433 2001
158.1'28—dc21
00-050256

This publication is designed to provide accurate and authoritative information with
regard to the subject matter covered. It is sold with the understanding that the publisher
is not engaged in rendering legal, accounting, or other professional advice. If legal advice
or other expert assistance is required, the services of a competent professional person
should be sought.
—From a *Declaration of Principles* jointly adopted by a Committee of the
American Bar Association and a Committee of Publishers and Associations

Cover illustration by Marcie Hawthorne.

This book is available at quantity discounts for bulk purchases.
For information, call 1-800-872-5627.

This book is dedicated to the members of the *Heartwarmers.com* online community who rallied behind the first Heartwarmers book and let us know they wanted to read more. They continue to bless us with a steady stream of fabulous stories, many of which have been chosen for this book.

To join the Heartwarmers mailing list, published five times weekly, send an e-mail to *join@heartwarmers.com* or visit the Web site at *www.heartwarmers4u.com*.

First Date

Hollingsworth McMillion's call light went on. I was a student nurse working the 3–11 shift; he was assigned to me for patient care. I went to his room to answer the call.

He had received shoulder surgery the day before, and I had not yet met him. The status report at the beginning of the shift indicated that he was a single male recuperating without problems. "This will be simple," I thought. "He probably wants fresh water."

There he was, sitting on his bed, smiling at me in an enchanting, mischievous sort of way. Well, that look not only caught me off guard, but it was tugging intriguingly on my heartstrings. And I, in turn, just had to make a good impression by presenting myself with the grace of a most efficient nurse.

My words got jumbled. I tripped over the tray table and fumbled, trying to keep the water pitcher from splashing to the floor. All that grace and efficient nurse stuff had flown out the window; I was acting like a space cadet of a schoolgirl.

1

Seemingly, he ignored my predicament, although I dare say he enjoyed every minute of it. Never letting go of that smile, he softly said, "The doctor said I could get up and walk around with my arm in a sling."

Sling . . . sure, I could do that—with my eyes closed.

I checked his chart. The order had been written during the day shift, and I wondered why they hadn't taken care of it. Anyway, I was glad, as this was my chance to redeem myself with professional composure in front of him.

There I am in his room with the triangle cravat thing that was the only offering for a sling back in the 1960s. There he is, still sitting there with that same smile. And there I am trying to put that thing on his arm. I had it upside down, downside up, sideways, and every way but the right way.

He never said a word, just kept smiling at me as he placed the sling correctly on his own arm. Well, I did tie it around his neck right. I think! Embarrassed? I was downright red-faced mortified. I never exited a patient's room so fast, praying I didn't fall flat on my face doing it!

For the rest of the shift it was a must for me to avoid him. I just knew he thought I was an absolute idiot. I bet he was going to have a laughing fine time telling his police colleagues about having to show the nurse how to do her job!

Finally, the interminable shift was over. I couldn't wait to get back to the dorm. The head nurse thought someone should escort me, as I was the only student on duty. I declined, saying I had walked around the block many times before at night by myself with no problem. Actually, that was a lie, but she just wasn't going to understand my need of putting hasty distance between myself and Mr. Shoulder Surgery Patient.

So there I was, walking around the block to the dorm, breathing a sigh of relief, when I heard footsteps behind me. My heart started pounding. Apparently the head nurse was wrong. I figured another student must have been on duty on another floor. I turned to see who it was.

Oh, my gosh! I could not believe my eyes. There he was! Arm in sling, bedroom slippers, dressed in street clothes . . . and smiling that smile.

I was flabbergasted! This guy was out on the street with me when he was supposed to be in the hospital, being a patient! I was too stunned to get any words out.

"Just wanted to make sure you got home alright." That's all he said as he walked with me. Safe or not, all I could envision was being kicked out of nursing school because a patient left the hospital with me. Who was going to believe my innocence in all this?

"You can't be out here. Go back now!" I don't know how many times I repeated that. He just kept following me and smiling that smile.

Finally we got to the dorm, and he said, "Everybody calls me Worth." Then, in the silence, for one moment, our eyes met. Humiliation and slings and being kicked out of school were forgotten. It was magnetic, that moment.

"I'll go back now that you're safe," Worth whispered, and he walked slowly away.

I whispered back, "Good night."

There were many things I did not know that night. Worth had put much effort into the entire evening. So much effort it needed to be called our first date. When he saw me come back on duty, he summoned the head nurse, a friend of his. He requested that she assign him to me for patient care and made her put away the sling she was going to put on his arm—because he wanted me to learn how to do it. And he instructed her to make sure I knew that he was single.

Two years later, we became husband and wife. Our marriage has turned out to be anything but ordinary, with Worth and his never-ending quirky adventures.

Our first date should have prepared me!

—GLORIA MCMILLION

After 35 years of marriage, Gloria has plenty of "Worth" stories to tell. And Worth probably has a few "Gloria" ones he could relate also. They continue to live in Amelia, Virginia, where they enjoy the outdoors and good neighbors.

My Mother's Magic Sandwich

To the simple observer, it may look like two pieces of bread, a tomato, and a couple of slabs of lunchmeat. But to me, sandwiches made by my mother are a masterpiece, almost suitable for framing.

From the time I can remember, I've always loved my mom's sandwiches. When I was a little girl, the only one who could create the ideal ham sandwich was my mommy. I've eaten in fancy restaurants, lived overseas, and traveled extensively. It's been proven. The whole world over, there isn't anybody in this solar system who can make a ham sandwich better than my mom can.

Still now, twenty years later, whenever I'm at my mom's house, if she's feeling up to it and I've timed it just right, she'll make me a sandwich. We'll go to the grocery store together and I'll observe her buying the sliced ham, carefully selecting a juicy tomato, and scouring over the hard rolls searching for the finest one. I'm in awe. How does she magically buy the most delicious, succulent, and perfect? They all look the same to me. But never fail, my mom *always* gets the best!

Back at her house, she nimbly cuts the bread; slices the ripe, red tomato at exactly the right place; and delicately places the meat in between. She intuitively adjusts the seasonings, carefully calculating the precise amount of salt and pepper I desire, and then masterfully puts the sandwich together. She serves it to me on a plate and behold, I am in the presence of culinary greatness.

Had I stood right beside her and done exactly the same steps, I would be able to tell which sandwich my mom made and which was the imposter sandwich. Try as I might, I just can't make a sandwich like my mom can.

Thankfully, part of the genetic code has been passed on. As a mother of three sons, I have somehow developed my own specialty. As basic as a mere sandwich may seem to some, my children have found an even easier food that only their mother can make perfectly—spaghetti. Not the fancy, robust Italian sauce passed down from generations. We're talking plain spaghetti noodles—the kind you just put into boiling water! For my boys, it appears that I have been anointed by God to make the world's best-cooked pasta. The mere mention of a spaghetti dinner sets my boys to dancing and prancing, with a veritable explosion of compliments flying from their lips.

Lest you think that my boys dance and prance for all of my delectable meals, I should set the record straight. One memorable moment stands out as a reminder that, perhaps, I should just stick with simple spaghetti if I wish to earn their favor.

After several months of annoying body aches and pains, a friend suggested I start taking vitamins and some organic, unrefined oils to aid in my overall health. I was interested in getting myself back into better shape and so it didn't take much to convince me. Once I began using them, I liked the results, so I faithfully took the five capsules every day until the time came when I needed refills.

While looking through the mail order catalog for the product, I was delighted to find another product any good mother would want to give her children. I found the children's version of these oil pills I had been taking. I carefully read the description and without hesitation placed my order.

Soon the small box arrived at our doorstep, just before my two oldest boys arrived home from school. My freshly baked brownies were cooling on the kitchen counter. I looked at the colorful bottle their special product had arrived in, and a secret plan started cooking in my head. Darling little jungle animals decorated the bottle. Big, bold lettering emphasized the scrumptious butterscotch flavor. A caption said it was delicious over desserts! I swept into action.

My guys bounded up the street and took their usual places around the kitchen table, eagerly awaiting their afternoon snack. I told them about the yummy brownies, and they were practically salivating with anticipation! Carefully, I cut each of my three sons a square of warm brownie, and then I added the secret ingredient. I diverted their attention and poured a few thick teaspoons of this oil on top of their brownies. The oil sat there on the brownies for a moment, almost like it was saying, "Are you SURE you want to do this?" but then it seeped deep into the dark chocolate.

They'd never know I had added some health food in the middle of this treat. Ah ha! Mission accomplished!

I presented each boy with his own plate. It was Nathaniel, the oldest (age nine) and most discerning, who asked me, "Mom, what's that on the brownies?" I gingerly walked around the question and encouraged him to dig in. The bite had barely entered his mouth when he grimaced and contorted. He held the moist brownie bits on the curl of his tongue, hoping not to swallow any, and cried, "Ugh! Mom, these are sick! What did you do? They taste terrible!"

I tried not to laugh, and despite me encouraging him to try another bite (he was almost gagging from the first one), he quickly declined. Seeing their big brother so grossed out, the other boys suddenly lost interest in their snack. They scrambled from the table before their mother could torture them, as she had their brother.

I wanted to be the best mom in the world with a homemade snack and some health food all rolled up into one great afternoon treat. My attempts to sneak more nutrition into their meals were continually foiled. The tofu I added to their tacos was a bomb. The seitan (mashed soybean curd) I tried to present as chicken was a culinary calamity. I even tried spinach brownies—again, less than popular with the troops.

While the taste of that nasty brownie concoction will hopefully fade from my son's mind and palate one day, I take solace in knowing that he'll probably grow up remembering one thing— that his mom made a mean plate of spaghetti!

My own mother didn't hit the mark with everything she made—please, let's not even talk about the escarole soup! But one thing's for sure, she never made a bad sandwich.

We mothers can rest assured that although we may not be remembered for all of the grand meals we made, it's the everyday, commonplace love that is never forgotten. I bite down on my mother's tender, tasty sandwich, and my sons devour their mother's slippery noodles, and we feel loved once again.

—CINDY M. WINTER-HARTLEY

Once a popular public speaker and trainer, Cindy M. Winter-Hartley is now the contented wife and stay-at-home mother of three sons. She lives in North Carolina with her mother and although she bravely struggles with fibromyalgia and other related illnesses, Cindy's mom can always find time to make her a lunch she will never forget. Her family is the source of many stories and much inspiration.

What Can a Dime Say?

THERE WAS ALWAYS SOMETHING SPECIAL ABOUT OUR RELATIONSHIP. My father and I both knew what the other was thinking. We usually enjoyed the same activities. As a child, I ran to him with all of my troubles. Many nights, I crawled into his lap. His gentle hands rubbed my back, and his steady rocking put me to sleep. My dreams were peaceful, simply because I knew that my daddy was close by.

When my hormones began to rage as a teenager, somehow Daddy understood that, too. He listened when I confided in him. He encouraged me when I was down. He didn't always allow me to do many of the things that I wanted to do. Curfews and rules were strictly enforced. His rules were endorsed with love, however. Even though I didn't always like the rules, down deep, I understood them. He saw to that.

When I became a young woman, he offered needed advice, but only when I asked. He helped me through many difficult and trying times. He welcomed my children into the world and loved them dearly. I depended on Daddy's wisdom. There was no doubt in my mind that as long as he was living on this earth, I had nothing to fear. He would stand beside me, through thick and thin. We never parted without a hug, a kiss, and a sincere "I love you."

Suddenly, one day, I awoke to the fact that my daddy was getting sick. I tried to deny his illness for as long as I could. The day that he was placed into a nursing facility marks one of the worst days of my life. That night, I cried myself to sleep. Quickly, Daddy's mind left him. I wanted desperately to dance with him, hold him, and make some sense of our conversations. Daddy stared blankly toward the ceiling as I talked to him.

Suddenly, frightening words entered our family's vocabulary. "Parkinson's," "Alzheimer's," "dementia," and "high blood pressure" became a part of our everyday language. The day that "terminal" joined the unpleasant list of words opened up another set of horrifying emotions.

Despite the doctor's grim diagnosis, Daddy lived three and a half years longer than expected. That extended time gave me the opportunity to hug him, wash his face, and offer him many cool drinks of water.

Saying "I love you" was a privilege and an honor for me. I'm grateful for every single visit that I had with him during those trying years.

"He's hanging on for you," a friend told me one time. I wanted desperately for him to get well. I couldn't let him go. I did everything humanly possible to help him. "You need to place him in the hands of God," she said.

While I thought I had done just that many times before, I discovered one Sunday afternoon that I hadn't.

That day, my family and I entered his nursing home room, like we had done many times before. It was obvious that Daddy was much worse than he had been a couple of days earlier. I asked him for a kiss. He puckered his lips bigger than he had in years. My entire family commented on how big and unusual that kiss was for him.

"I love you, Daddy," I whispered.

"I love you, too," he mouthed. I was elated. For three years, he hadn't even called my name. He rarely spoke. But that day, he said my favorite words: "I love you, too."

In less than 10 minutes something unexplainable happened. An unusual attack hit him. As the hospice nurse called it, he entered the dying process, shortly after that final kiss. That night, after seeing him in severe pain, God gave me the courage to finally let him go. Exactly one week later, Daddy left this world, while I rubbed his back. Sorrow filled my heart immensely, but a sense of peace was also present, as I knew that he was no longer suffering.

That night at the funeral home, Daddy expressed his love to me one more time. My family gathered there together. My brother opened his wallet.

For years, Daddy had said that he wanted a particular dime to be placed into his pocket after he died. Upon Daddy's instructions, my brother granted his wish and pulled out the dime, which meant so much to him.

Everyone in my family wanted to see it. We all wanted to know what was so special about that particular 10-cent piece. I cried when my brother announced that it was a 1955 dime. "It represents the year that Nancy was born," he said. Tears flowed down my cheeks as I remembered how happy Daddy told me he was to become the father of a little girl.

"I love you, too," I whispered before I left the funeral home that night.

I'll never know why he loved me so much, but I'm so thankful that he did.

Daddy knew many years earlier that I would need an extra loving word after he was gone. In his own special way, with a single dime, he shared his heartfelt love with me one last time.

What can a dime say? It can say a mouthful when a woman's heart is shattered over the loss of a very special man, whom she had loved for her entire lifetime. I never knew that money could talk. But this dime spoke loudly and clearly to me, "I love you!"

—NANCY GIBBS

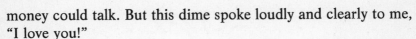 *Nancy believes that if her Dad could share a few words of wisdom with us today, these are the words he would say: "If you have good health, appreciate it. If you love someone, let them know. Freely give to others, as you have been given. Life is for the living. Live your lives to the fullest until we meet again." Nancy is doing just that.*

Marriage Made in Heaven

I WAS WALKING DOWN THE HALL OF THE DORM MY FRESHMAN YEAR AT college when I first met Jon. He and Steph, a friend of mine, were standing outside her door. Jon's hair was tousled, his shoulders were slumped, and his hands were buried deep in the pockets of his patchwork jeans. I said hello to Steph as I approached and nodded in his direction.

"Hello, Connie, do you know Jon?" Steph asked me. "His dad is the head of the music department here at school."

As she spoke my eyes drank in the sight before me. Jon had beautiful deep brown eyes and his eyelashes were so long that they nearly swept the lenses of his small wire-framed glasses. He had perfectly shaped lips, and peeping just above the edge of his beard was a heart-capturing set of dimples.

"Hi, nice to meet you," I said, adding some excuse about an appointment. I continued my journey down the hall, never expecting to see him again. His dad was a professor and I was a country girl, our paths would probably never cross.

Somewhere deep inside me, though, the thrill of that first meeting nested and made itself at home.

By December my life was busy, as I threw myself into school and all the activities I loved. On top of classes and my job, I worked at the campus radio station and stayed involved in several organizations.

I was also struggling with a long-distance relationship that was going sour. I finally realized that I had not allowed God or my faith to influence any of my dating choices. My boyfriend and I were talking about marriage. I called to invite him to a special conference on prayer. He told me that he did not believe in my God or my religion.

I was at first surprised and hurt; then I was ashamed. Why had I not seen this coming? How could I, a preministerial student, have wasted so much time? We never spoke again.

Late one night I was sitting on my bed still numb, still hearing his voice telling me that he loved me, not my God. My God was the very essence of my being; how could he not see this? I sat for a long time, praying about my hurt and shame. I prayed that God would help me find a husband who would be right for me as a Christian minister.

It was bitter cold outside but my room felt stuffy and confining, so I bundled up and went out for a walk. After hours of walking and praying, suddenly, I was not alone.

"What are you doing out here in the cold at four A.M.?" A voice shattered my silence.

I whirled around and there stood Jon, his hair still tousled, his hands shoved down in his pockets, and his brown eyes shining. We walked together and talked until sunrise.

Could God have answered my prayers so quickly? That thrill inside me was awakened. I knew this boy was very special.

The next semester I began a new routine that forced our paths to cross regularly. I was a shameless flirt. One day I was joking around and stole Jon's keys. He chased me all around the dorm, and once outside, cornered me against the fence. I stood there acting so shy and innocent after weeks of plotting, planning, and flirting. He had me blocked up against the fence. His arms were just millimeters from an embrace, his feet were planted firmly in front of my toes, and his face was just a fraction of an inch away from my own. I could not blink without brushing against him.

Feelings emerged that I had never felt before. I was filled with excitement and fear. I was at once shy and bold. My mind was racing, *what's he going to do next?*

"Give me my keys," he ordered.

"Make me!"

"I might."

"Oh sure, let's see you."

"Connie," he said; then he softly kissed my ear. I turned the other way, averting my eyes.

"Connie," he repeated; then he kissed my other ear. I tried to shift but I couldn't move. "Connie."

He kissed me again and again until I managed to squeeze out a feeble "what?"

"Will you go out with me?"

"Where?"

"Pizza and a movie."

"When?"

"Tomorrow at seven."

"Yes."

"Good. I'll need my keys. See you tomorrow."

Those days seem so long ago. We have been married twenty-two years, and now have three teenage children. Yet sometimes today, he touches me, kisses me, or speaks my name in such a way that I can feel the fence at my back again.

I am not a princess, and he is not a knight in shining armor. We have both been dirty, angry, depressed, confused, sick, and ugly.

But I still tremble when he holds my hand, and I still melt inside when he softly kisses my ear. He loves me the way God intended me to be loved. I am glad that I finally released my love life to God's tender, strong hand.

—CONNIE WOOLDRIDGE

Connie is a United Methodist Licensed Local Pastor. She is currently serving Grandview United Methodist in Winfield, Kansas, and attending seminary. Connie's husband Jon is a computer instructor at a college nearby. Their eldest daughter, Lindy, is beginning a college career as an art major. Joannie and Joseph are students in Winfield Sr. and Jr. High schools.

My Self-Esteem Lifter

I HAVE JUST GRADUATED FROM EIGHTH GRADE, A MOST MEMORABLE year, as middle school tends to be for most young adults. Years from now, I'll probably have forgotten most of the assignments given to me by my teachers. But one assignment, I will never forget.

I was asked to write a paper about my number one hero in life. I didn't have to agonize long about who it should be. It is my best friend, Ryan. I guess it does sound a little weird when I say that my best friend is my number one hero. But, I feel that the ability to change someone's life is definitely a hero's ability. He fits all the criteria I've set up for a hero. He's kind, generous, helpful, nice, brave, gentle (in his own boy way), adventurous, and he always practices what he preaches.

Ryan sets the right example for all of the younger kids at my school, and for a lot of older people, too. Ryan is judgmental like all people are, but he looks at a person's morals, a person's heart and actions. Those are the things he sees before he sees looks, or weight, or hair, or color. To be such a good person with all the right qualities makes him my special hero.

I never had a lot of good times at my school, St. John's. Especially when it came to peer-to-peer relationships. I was the overweight kid in class, thus, I was always being made fun of. Even though I knew I was a good person on the inside, I could never forget about my outside. I was always being reminded of how unattractive my peers thought I was. I hated going to school because I feared the relentless personal attacks and teasing I endured.

It's not easy being the different kid, in their eyes, the weird kid who doesn't talk like everyone else, or act like them, or, sadly, look like them. It's been that way for me since I was a little girl, first entering school. But my hatred of school, and of myself, all changed in the fifth grade. And it's because of my hero, Ryan.

Ryan was being teased all the time by the same kids who teased me. He walked differently—he had an unusual bounce to his step that made it look like he was skipping when he walked. He also had a difficult family situation. He lived with his grandmother, who has permanent custody of him and his two sisters. Like me, Ryan didn't have friends, so he sat at the corner or on the end of the lunch table and didn't talk to anybody.

Unlike me, Ryan didn't let it get to him. He was perpetually happy, whether kids teased him or not. In some ways, that made the kids tease him more, but he didn't care.

We became instant friends. We each stopped eating alone at lunchtime. We laughed and talked, all day long. Over time, I learned that Ryan liked me for what was inside of me, and that really increased my self-esteem.

After Ryan became my friend, the teasing didn't seem so bad. I knew if I looked at Ryan I could laugh because of some funny face he made or an inside joke between us. The kids kept on teasing me, just like they always did. But because of Ryan's friendship, I began to feel better about myself and less shy. Ryan taught me that not everyone was like the classmates that made fun of me.

I was one of the few girls in the whole eighth grade with no boyfriend yet, or ever for that matter. One day, I went into a deep "no one likes me" mood. I went back to Ryan's house to hang out, hoping my mood would change. I cried to Ryan about no boy liking me and how much that hurt. "I like you," Ryan replied.

"Yeah, but would you go out with me?" I moped.

Ryan responded, "I am here, and I'm not going anywhere."

He was absolutely right; he hasn't gone anywhere. Ryan is still my best friend, and he always will be. Anyway, I'd rather have a best friend like Ryan than a boyfriend any day!

After my teacher read my hero report she added to the bottom of the paper in bright blue ink, "You are so fortunate to have each other. Take care of your friendship, it is a vessel that will take you many places."

I count my blessings every day that Ryan is my shipmate. His positive attitude toward life is rubbing off on me.

—ALISON RICCARDI

Harry Emerson Fosdick once said: "Friends are necessary to a happy life. When friendship deserts us we are as lonely as a ship, left by the tide high upon the shore. When friendship returns to us, it is as though the tide came back, gave us buoyancy and freedom, and opened us to the wide places of the world."

Of this, Alison says: "Ryan is more than the tide for me, he is the wind that keeps me sailing on and on." Alison was delighted to find out, upon sharing her heroes report with Ryan, that she is one of Ryan's heroes, too.

The Tree Swing

GROWING UP THE "BABY" OF THE FAMILY, I WAS ALWAYS MONITORED and protected by my older siblings. My two brothers, Pat and Don, and my sister, Linda, were 8 to 11 years my senior. They would always come to my rescue, whisking me away before the hand of my mother, or anyone else for that matter, found its target at the seat of my pants.

I came to rely on my brothers and sisters for my protection when I found myself in distressing predicaments. Whenever I was picked on by anyone, whether deserved or not, I often relied on the old line, "I'm gonna tell my big brothers and sister on you and you'll be sorry!"

It seemed to work every time. Linda, Pat, and Don were gentle, kind, and fun-loving teenagers, except when it came to sticking up for their little kid sister.

Life was simpler in the fifties. As children growing up in the country, we created our own entertainment, all of it outdoors. Most of our joys were very simple, compared to today's standards. Watching the black-and-white TV was not what we considered having fun. We were life's participants, not spectators.

One summer day, Linda spotted the perfect branch for a tree swing across the road from our house. On a big old oak tree, she and my brothers strung up a beautiful, strong tree swing with a huge thick rope and a great wood seat. It was perfect. My young friends and I would take turns swinging and enjoying our very own playground. Life was good.

One particular day three teenage neighborhood bullies came over to "our playground" and ordered my friends and I to get off of the swing. They instructed us that they were taking it over and from now on we would have to ask them for permission to use it.

That was a very big mistake. They obviously did not know with whom they were dealing. I had a powerful backup system. I told them I was telling my big sister and brothers on them and that they were really gonna get it. They pushed me off the swing, mocking me with the typical, "nah nah, nah nah, nah, nah." I retreated, threatening, "You'll be sorry!"

My brothers, Pat and Don, were not home that afternoon, but Linda was. My friends and I ran to my home, sobbing and crying hysterically, wailing, "The mean boys will not let us use our own swing."

I could see my sister becoming indignant and angry as she listened to our major life predicament. She had had run-ins with those characters before, but now they were messing with her little sister. That was the wrong thing to do.

Just the response I was hoping for. I had ignited the fuse.

I knew she would go tell them a thing or two. But I was wrong. Instead, she opened up the kitchen drawer and pulled out a big butcher knife. My eyes grew big. I knew those boys were in for trouble. I thought, "Oh no, I should not have tattled!"

Tugging at my sister's shirt, I tried to stop her by telling her it was OK, that we would just let them have the swing, but she brushed me aside and stormed out the door with the knife clenched tightly in her fist. My friends and I followed close behind, terrified of what was about to take place.

As my sister approached the three boys, who were of course much older and bigger than she was, she demanded that they get off of our swing.

Laughing, they sneered, "Oh yeah? And who is going to make us?" She responded very assertively, "I am. If the little ones can't play on it, no one will. Now get off!"

The bullies refused to budge. She calmly said, "I gave you a chance." It was a fifties-style version of Clint Eastwood's famous line, "Make my day!" I closed my young eyes, thinking the worst was about to happen, and it would all be my fault. I didn't want to witness it.

Against their loud protests of "HEY, YOU CAN'T DO THAT!" she calmly confirmed, "I just did." I had opened my eyes in time to see Linda climb the tree and hack down the swing, sending the two boys on it leaping for safety as it came crashing to the ground.

My friends and I watched in silence from the sidelines. As the drama unfolded and we realized that no one was going to die, we began cheering her on. When she climbed back down from the tree the bullies stood there in amazement as she faced them off. With feet firmly planted and hands on hips, she told them they better leave.

About that time Pat and Don returned home, wondering what all the commotion was about. My front line was moving in. Linda replied that the boys were just leaving. As they retreated, they assured my brothers that, "Everything is cool, man!"

It was like a scene from *West Side Story*.

Those ornery boys had just tormented the wrong little kid. My sister became our hero that day. She replaced the swing in the same spot and we were never disturbed again.

Last year I brought this story to Linda's recollection because it has always held a special place in my heart. She was dying of cancer. She beamed when I reminisced about the time when she backed down the bullies single-handedly. She liked me to repeat the story over and over to each visitor that came by. It made her laugh and gave her hope, remembering a time when she had the power to fight off bullies, just as she was confronting the biggest bully of her life.

Linda passed away August 1, 1999. I promised her before her death that I would write the story about one of the times when she was my hero and all was well. Several months later, I was clearing out an old drawer and found a pretty card she had sent me ten years ago. She wrote: "Always remember the good times." I will. Thanks to the protection and love of my older sister and brothers, my childhood memories are filled with good times.

—ROSE GORDON

Rose Gordon is living in Granger, Indiana, with her husband, John, and their miniature pinscher, Mincher. They also enjoy spending time at their home in the Blue Ridge Mountains in North Carolina. She is currently working on her private pilot's license. Her brothers, Pat and Don, continue to reside nearby, and they remain close.

$\mathcal{J}$ust in the Nick of Time

MARRIAGE, BY ITS VERY NATURE, COULD BE DESCRIBED AS AN ADVENTURE. It's full of challenges, frustrations, harrowing moments, and, if you're lucky, occasional excitement. My marriage is like any other in that regard. My nerve-wracking, nail-biting, teeth-gnashing adventure came from the way I got married.

Roger and I, ages 29 and 27 respectively, had been dating almost two years, much of it long distance. We had lived together for a few months, but he was hesitant to make the final commitment. Many of our friends were taking the plunge and exerting a less-than-subtle peer pressure on us. I was impatiently waiting for him to finally pop the question.

On November 18, 1991, Roger and I had gotten together to watch Monday Night Football. Our married friends were razzing us about our fear of wedlock. "Oh you'll never get married, you cowards!" they teased us.

How soon they'd eat those words.

When we got home that evening, Roger finally did it. He popped the question. Well, it was more like, "So, whattya think, should we get married?" Was he proposing because his friends were riding him or because he was feeling that warm I-love-you glow that comes after a few beers?

I quickly decided it didn't matter. I wanted to be married to him and so I said "YES" before he could change his mind. We immediately began planning. After taking such a remarkable step in the right direction, we wanted to keep the momentum going. We decided we'd go to the courthouse next week to apply for a marriage license—heck, we'd even get married right then and there.

Yeah, that's good. "But, if we're going so soon," we reasoned, "why not just go tomorrow?"

Tomorrow?! Yeah.

Of course, there were lots of good reasons why we shouldn't get married the next day, like, we both had to work, and the courthouse closed at 4:00 P.M., and Roger had to have proof of his divorce, which was inconveniently stashed 10 miles away in the bank's safe-deposit box, and so on.

But being impetuous fools, we decided to do it anyway. Having made up our minds, it seemed unnecessary to go through months of preparations and planning. Somehow it made the whole wedding day seem more fun—not only would we prove to people that we did have the courage and commitment to get married, but we'd also do it at record speed.

Our decision made, Roger went to sleep and I tossed and turned most of the night. I wondered if it was all a giant practical joke he was playing on me, a trait he is known for. And I wondered how I could possibly love a man that could sleep at a time like this! Sleep finally came for me, but it was a restless night.

When I stumbled into the kitchen to get my coffee the next morning, my mom, who had been staying with us while on an extended vacation, was sitting stunned at the kitchen table. Roger was across from her, grinning like an idiot. I knew in an instant that he had told her of our decision. I was hugely relieved on one hand, as I knew then that he *did* intend to honor his commitment. I was also relieved that he took on the burden of dropping the bomb on my mom.

Would she think I was pregnant or a complete fool? All of this flashed through my mind in nanoseconds, but before I could even open my mouth to speak, my mom grabbed me in a huge hug and congratulated me. After a few minutes of giddiness and giggling, we all became quite matter-of-fact about the whole affair. There were considerable logistics to address and our other witness (Roger's mother) to inform. I left that task to him, gave him a quick kiss, and hurried off to work, where I was needed to train a class.

Keeping my composure (and a coherent train of thought) while instructing my students was difficult, but keeping the secret was even worse! We had agreed we wouldn't tell anyone else until we were officially married. My coworkers Jackie and Kelly, pretty close friends, knew something was up, but they could not drag it out of me. Midmorning I received a call from Roger's boss. He told me that he had heard a *lot* of creative excuses for needing to leave work early, but Roger's had taken the cake. He wanted to hear it from me that we really were getting married. I told him I could hardly believe it myself.

I barely made it until 2:30 P.M., when I let my grateful students leave early so I could pick up my mom. When I got to my house, it was only 3:00 P.M., and I felt comfortable, knowing we had plenty of time. The courthouse is within 10 miles of my home. Since it was pre–rush hour, we hopped on I-95.

We were cruising along merrily for the first five miles. Aside from some jittery nerves, I was pretty composed and relaxed.

Then, drumroll please . . . we saw the glaring red glow of at least a million brake lights ahead. The composure slipped a few notches. Mom sensed my increased anxiety and reminded me that it could be any little old thing, like a trooper with someone pulled over. I tried to control the feelings of dread and impending doom that were overtaking me. And it wasn't about the thought of getting married—it was about the thought of missing it!

I looked at my watch every ten seconds. It was 3:20. "Ok, we're all right, we should still be there in time," I reassured myself.

I spent the next 35 minutes stuck in traffic, screaming and cursing at the fools who chose *my* wedding day to meet in a crunch of twisted metal. I was afraid my beloved would think I stood him up. The bride-to-be was doubled over with agonizing stomach cramps, headache, and nausea.

At 3:55 P.M. we were still on I-95. We could see our exit about 100 yards ahead but couldn't quite get there. I announced to my mom that I was going to do the rest on foot. At the bottom of the ramp, I explained to her, I'd flag down someone who'd take me to the courthouse, a scant three blocks to the east.

My mom probably thought I had lost my mind when she learned of our sudden decision to marry. Now she protested vociferously, her last chance to talk some sense into her crazed daughter.

But a bride's gotta do what a bride's gotta do. I opened the car door.

Just then, as if a giant invisible hand had reached down and started pushing the logjam free, traffic began moving. I yanked my foot back into the car as we rocketed down the off-ramp. Mom ran the red light at the intersection and raced toward the courthouse. As we screeched to a halt in front of the courthouse, the time was 4:01.

I jumped out of the car and raced for the double doors. I grabbed the handle of the right side and pulled. It was *locked!* In a gesture of fury and frustration, I grabbed both handles and yanked. I must have had some adrenaline rush, because the door opened in front of me. I hurtled over the divider rope separating me from Roger, who was forlornly sitting on a bench in front of the marriage license counter. As I feared, he was thinking the worst. He swept me into his arms and asked what had taken me so long.

Despite my resolve to be stoic, I started to cry. I feared that this was some sort of omen, a message that our union was doomed from the start. I thought I might just throw up from all the stress and wracked nerves. So rather than trying the impossible, to put it all together in words, I just wailed. My mom, after parking the car, was able to tell the story for me.

The marriage license staff felt so sorry for us that they performed the wedding despite the late hour. While I had pretty much regained control, I honestly think they were afraid of my having a complete breakdown if they refused us.

A lovely lady named Michelle married us, using beautiful vows she had written herself. While I still was feeling a little shaky, I was calmed by how unflappable and steady Roger was. His voice quivered a little as we exchanged vows, but overall he was completely composed. My mom and mother-in-law (who was later than me, incidentally) were beaming. I knew if we could get through this trial, the rest would be manageable—maybe even fun.

It's been almost nine years since that day. Our friends and family members were shocked when we told them what we had done. If my mother hadn't witnessed it, she probably wouldn't have believed it either. Never for a second have we doubted that we made the right decision. We chose an unorthodox way to get married, but we like it that way. If there's a road less traveled, it's the one we are compelled to take. And the fun of surprising people so completely has almost compensated for the gut-wrenching terror I felt for much of my wedding day.

Emphasis on the almost.

Looking back at the emotions of that day, the stress and the terror, I have to laugh at my narrow perspective. Knowing what I do now, what I really should have feared is not the event itself, but what accompanies married life—the in-law relationships, the mortgage payment, the kids!

Happily for us, the adventure continues.

—STACY BERGER

Stacy Berger, her husband, Roger, and their sons, RJ and Jamie, lead a fairly exciting life of lizard catching, bass fishing, and boat watching in West Palm Beach, Florida. Stunned-but-supportive moms Susan and Patricia still live nearby and happily spoil the grandkids rotten.

Stacy is a Vice President of Human Resources at one of the nation's largest banks, as well as the owner of a fledgling small business. She also enjoys writing when she can find the time.

$\mathcal{A}$ Dream Come True

THE VERY FIRST DAY THAT I MET MY HUSBAND, ROY, HE SHARED WITH me his lifelong dream to become a teacher. While he attended college immediately after high school, he allowed other things to interfere with his goal and failed to take the classes required. After having his transcript evaluated, he learned that he needed to attend school for eighteen more months in order to receive a master's degree and to obtain the certificate that would allow him to teach.

Only a couple of months after we met, we became husband and wife. For several years, my heart's desire was to help my sweetheart reach his goal.

At the beginning of each school year, Roy wore a sad expression. I was determined that I would do something to help him become the teacher that he wanted so desperately to be. But the time slowly passed by, and year after year, his dream seemed to become more impossible.

With three children and a mortgage, the funds were low and the idea of Roy going back to college remained only a dream. Six years passed by very quickly. It was obvious that his heart was not in his current job. While he was making enough money to pay the bills and to enable me to remain a stay-at-home mom, I could tell that he was not happy with his career in retail management.

The day came when I dropped my youngest child, Becky, off at school for the first time. I had time during the day for the first time in years, to do with as I wished. I decided as I pulled out of the parking lot that I would make Roy's dream become a reality. I would find a job that would help pay his college tuition and buy his books.

A few years earlier, a friend mentioned in casual conversation that a benefit of working at a local university was free tuition for the employee and his or her immediate family members. That sounded like a dandy place for me to apply first. After I dropped Becky off at school, I dried the motherly tears, returned home, and pulled a business suit out of the closet that I hadn't worn in a very long time. It still fit, although I had to hold my breath to button the skirt! I proceeded to the university personnel office.

I had not even discussed my idea with Roy. I wanted to surprise him.

I took several tests and interviewed for a secretarial position. The personnel director asked me why I wanted to work for the university. I explained my husband's desire to finish his education. Before the day was over, I was offered a job. I learned that he could start school tuition-free six months later.

Roy arrived home that evening, not having a clue that his life was about to change. I shared with him the events of my day and my plans for his future.

He stared at me in disbelief.

"Wait a minute. Now say that again," he said. "I'm going to be a teacher! Are you sure?"

"I start work next Monday," I replied. "You can start taking classes, for free, six months later."

He put his arms around me and hugged me warmly. "Thank you," he said. "Thank you so much."

"Daddy's going to be a teacher," Chad shouted. All three of the children cheered.

For the next couple of years we all worked very hard. In addition to my job at the university, I kept books for two other companies. Roy worked three jobs and began attending school full-time as soon as possible. He wrote term papers that I typed for him at night. My children helped at home in every way possible. Roy's dream to become a teacher became a family goal, not his alone. The completion of each quarter became a time to celebrate.

When Roy was about halfway through his course of study, the university changed its rules. Graduate students could no longer attend tuition-free.

Because of the large cost of the tuition at the private institution, he would be forced to drop out. I cried bitterly the day that I received the grim news. We had all worked so hard to get as far as we were. He made straight A's in spite of his busy schedule. I felt like the world had come to an end.

We just couldn't give up now, not after all we, and the kids, had been through to make this happen for Roy. With determination and every ounce of courage we could muster, Roy and I went to see the president of the university.

We poured our heart out to the man who sat behind his desk asking how he could help us. When we finished our impassioned plea, he signed a tuition waver form and handed it to us to return to financial aid. "Good luck," he said, as he shook Roy's hand. We both left his office with big grins on our faces. I wanted to hug this generous and kind man, but I withheld the gesture. With a simple signature, he had restored our dream.

The next few quarters passed quickly and graduation day finally arrived. I cried as I watched Roy receive his much-sought-after diploma. One month later he became a middle school teacher. A few years later, he received the prestigious award of countywide Teacher of the Year.

When a family pulls together, anything is possible.

—NANCY GIBBS

 *Roy shares: For the first several years of marriage, we concentrated on building a relationship, establishing a home, and raising three children.*

This was all in God's great plan for us. His hand was still guiding us and the dream was still alive. When Nancy told me that she had found a job that would allow me to return to school to work on my master's degree and become a teacher, I was elated. I realized that in God's good time, he had made a way. That way was not always easy, but we chose to travel it, and I am glad that we did.

I have discovered that a dream is much better if it is shared. Our vision was and is not that one person sees and leads while everyone else simply follows. Our vision is shared in that we pursued it side by side, as a team, as a family. Through our combined efforts, and with God's help, I graduated and started teaching. I am truly thankful to my wife, Nancy, and my children, Brad, Chad, and Becky, for helping me achieve my lifelong dream.

Haven of Comfort

DURING THE PAST TWO YEARS, I HAVE HAD TO SPEND MOST OF MY TIME lying in bed, recovering from two very serious back surgeries.

Our little Shih Tzu, Bandit, was completely puzzled as to why I never got out of bed. The Shih Tzus are very tiny dogs from China, tipping the scales at approximately 13 pounds. They usually have long hair that is almost always white in color with black markings, brown markings, or both. Their hair grows very long, right down to the floor, giving them the appearance of a dust mop.

As you can probably tell from his name, Bandit has fluffy white hair with a circle of black around each one of his eyes.

Since I became ill, Bandit missed his playtime and long walks. He also missed his rides in the car, as I would always take him with me to run my daily errands around town. He would hop up in the back window of the car and sit staring at the people in the car behind us. Bandit looked exactly like one of those little artificial dogs you see in people's cars, with the little head that nods up and down from the motion of the car. Many an onlooker would take a second look, not knowing whether Bandit was a real dog or not.

There was nothing left for our poor little Bandit to do but jump up on the bed and curl into my side. He would snuggle there for hours and hours while I scratched behind his ears. If I turned over, he turned over as well. We became extremely close during this long recovery period of mine.

About a year and a half later, I am now fully recovered. When I get up each morning, Bandit and I go out for his first walk of the day. Upon returning, Bandit sits by the side of my already made bed, not understanding why we both aren't going back to lie down. Many times during the day I will find him sitting by the bedroom door as if to say, "Is it time to go to bed yet?"

Come evening, after the kitchen is cleaned and I sit down to watch a little TV, he won't give me a moment's peace. He looks at me with those big round eyes as if to say, "All right, now I really want to go to bed."

After such dedicated companionship during my recovery, I find I cannot help but give in to my faithful friend.

Now, as the clock chimes 8:30 P.M., I call out, "Okay, Bandit, now it is time to go to bed." His tail starts to wag so hard, he appears to be wiggling all over. He takes off in a run toward the bedroom door, where he patiently awaits his master.

Besides getting a good night's sleep every night, I am keeping my dear little friend very happy in the spot he has learned to love. He had discovered over the past year and a half that my bed was a haven of comfort for him, where he was constantly cherished and showered with affection.

—PATTI JONES

 Patti Jones lives with her husband in Florida, where they enjoy a very active retired life of golf, clubs, reading, and just plain old socializing. She is a freelance writer and writes for a local newspaper. She also enjoys doing volunteer work. The biggest love in her life is her grandsons.

The Treasured Box

THE SUMMER OF 1987 HAD BEEN A LONG HOT SPELL, ONE OF THE longest summers I could remember. We were moving into the month of September, and with the cooling of the weather, a special event was about to happen for my family.

My wife, Donna, and I were anticipating the arrival of our first grandchild. Sheila, my oldest daughter, was due any day.

In times such as these, the telephone takes on a new importance. With each ring, we grabbed the receiver, as if it were about to jump off the cradle and go flying out the door before we had a chance to say hello.

Then the call finally came. It was my son-in-law Pat on the other end of the phone. "Dad," he announced, "we're going to the hospital, it's time!"

A few hours later, Danielle arrived into our world, a healthy, beautiful little girl.

As new grandparents, our lives had made a complete circle. Once again, there was a baby in our lives. Once again, as with all grandparents, we could relive the excitement of watching and being involved with a child growing up and learning all about life. We could spoil her rotten and not be blamed.

As Christmas approached that year, it once again found us in the toy stores, a place we had not been in years. Why is it that new grandparents want to buy everything in the store, when a four-month-old baby can only shake a rattle or bite on something? Why even pick up an Easy Bake Oven or a Barbie doll? Those toys are years away. But we thought about buying them anyway.

Christmas was joyous that year to be sure. Being active at church kept us very busy, and the added excitement of our new granddaughter on Christmas morning made that year one to remember.

Christmas came and went, and so did New Year's Eve, and then we moved into the "winter slump," a time when it seems like all you do is get though it and wait for springtime.

Early in January, Donna was having pains in her abdominal area. The pain finally became so unbearable, we brought Donna to the emergency room of the hospital. The medical staff took her to a room for an examination as I sat in a waiting room, waiting for the doctor to come and explain what was wrong with her.

I was not too worried. In this day of modern medicine they can fix almost anything. She was only 46 years old, how serious could it be?

After an hour or so the doctor came into the waiting room. "We have to admit her immediately," he said somberly. "She can't even go home to get a change of clothes." I was then instructed to wait until they got her into a room, and a specialist would come in and talk to us.

I was more concerned now, but I still wasn't panicking. I figured an operation of some sort was needed immediately, and then she'd be fixed. I waited and waited, for what seemed like an eternity. Then, finally, a nurse instructed me to go to my wife's room, where we would meet with a physician. My wife was as puzzled as I was. We had no idea what was wrong with her as we waited for the doctor to come in.

The doctor eventually entered the room, and without any hesitation in his voice at all, announced coldly, "Advanced liver cancer. There's absolutely nothing we can do and an operation at this point is useless." I vaguely remember some other words, like, he "would arrange to make her as comfortable in the final stages" as he could.

In that brief moment, our beautiful lives came crashing down.

The next few months were lived in such a confused state, I don't think either of us really believed it could or would happen. Final stages? Our minds could not comprehend that she was dying. We talked about it as if it was years off instead of months. The doctor said she had up to a year. How a doctor can predict that you have 365 days to live has always baffled me.

During the months that followed, Sheila would bring Danielle over to spend time with her grandma. Danielle was growing and becoming more active, while her grandma was failing rapidly. Donna would sit and hold Danielle and kiss her little face, and I would see the tears welling up in her eyes as she would say, "I will never get to see her grow up. She will never even remember me." My daughter and I assured her, "We will not let her forget who you are and how much you loved her."

Donna passed away on Friday, May 13, 1988. Four short months after her diagnosis. Our lives will never be the same. Keeping our promise to her, my daughter and I were determined to keep her memory alive.

Danielle was the only grandchild she ever held.

Through photographs and photo albums, stories, and memories, Danielle knows who her grandma was and how much she was loved by her. But I wanted more for her. Sorting through my wife's belongings after her passing, I took a little jewelry box that I had given her for Christmas that year, and wrapped it up and put it away. It was one of the few earthly possessions that she loved the minute she saw it. I knew that one day, when Danielle was old enough to take care of it, I would give it to her, because her grandmother treasured the little box and would have wanted her to have it.

The Christmas of 1998, 10 years after Donna's passing, I took the little jewelry box and wrapped it up as a present for Danielle. I wrote a poem for her and put it in a wooden frame that matched the wood of the jewelry box. I instructed her to open it with her mother when they were alone together. The jewelry box and the poem will forever keep the memory of her grandmother alive in her heart.

This is Danielle's poem.

"Treasured Box"
(Dedicated to Danielle)

I know it doesn't look like much, this little jewelry box,
It has no drawers to hold things in, and has no keys or
    locks.
It's small and it won't hold too much, inside the small
    glass door,
But holding jewelry isn't all this little box is for.

It has a meaning all its own, this little box of wood,
And now that you are old enough, I'll share it as I should.
I know that you will understand, now that you are eleven,
This was your Grandma's jewelry box, before she went to
    Heaven.

I bought this jewelry box for her, the same year of your birth,
But the Christmas of that year, was Grandma's last on earth.
You were her only grandchild, that she ever got to see,
The year I put this jewelry box under our Christmas tree.

Your Grandma went to Heaven, and I put this box away,
And kept it safe to give to you, some future Christmas Day.
I knew a Christmas Day would come, and now it's finally
    here.
I think you're old enough to have, the jewelry box this year.

As you read this little poem, please try not to be sad.
Your Grandma knows you have it now, and that will make
    her glad.
So, every time you open up this box I give to you,
Remember that your Grandma's fingers once opened it
    up too.

I know you don't remember, how she used to hold you tight,
The same way that she held your Mother, rocking her at
    night.
She held you in her arms, and watched you sleeping
    through her tears,
She knew her time was limited, while you had many years.

I know you only know her, from the pictures that we keep,
Now Grandma's safe in Heaven, and she'd not want you
 to weep.
I know what I am doing, is what she'd want me to do,
Because she loved this little box, and Grandma loves you too.

Now keep this little jewelry box, as safe as it can be.
Hide it in some secret place, or out where you can see.
Then, in the future, on the day when God gathers his
 flocks,
You'll see your Grandma, Donna, who left you this little box.
—JAMES A. KISNER

James and Danielle, now age 13, continue to have a close relationship. James has seven other grandchildren now, whom he adores and spends time supporting in their activities (such as baseball, softball, and live theater, and he even has two vocalists among them). He is known as "Poppy" to them all, a name that Danielle bestowed upon him when she first started talking. It is also the pen name he uses for his poetry.

ℒove at First Read

LEAVES FELL SLOWLY AS I WALKED THROUGH HARVARD SQUARE. IT WAS a perfect fall day in New England—almost. If only I had that man of my dreams with me, then it would be perfect. I was twenty-two and lonely for a partner.

But, I consoled myself, I had the next best thing—my best friend, Lynn. We worked in Boston together, and she had an apartment in Cambridge. We strolled to her place, gabbing away about—what else—men.

When we got to her apartment I crashed on the couch. She got on the phone, I assumed to talk with her new boyfriend. Next thing I knew, the phone was in my face.

"Talk," she ordered me. "Go on."

"Who is it?" I whispered.

She just smiled and shook the phone at me. I grabbed it reluctantly.

"Hello," I said tentatively.

"Hi. Is this Jennifer?" A strange man's voice echoed through the phone line. He sounded like he was far away.

"Yes. Who is this?"

"Jeff. I'm Lynn's friend. She just called me and told me I had to talk to you!" I glared at Lynn. She shrugged her shoulders.

"Ah, what are we supposed to talk about?" I stuttered. My heart was racing and it was hard getting the words out. He sounded nice, really nice.

"I don't know, but Lynn said you are the girl of my dreams."

"She did?" I glared harder at Lynn and felt the heat rise through my cheeks. She walked into the other room. "How embarrassing."

"I know. Lynn has a way of fixing people up." Jeff cleared his throat.

"Well, where do you live? Maybe we can get together," I asked, feeling more hopeful. Who knows, maybe Jeff is the man of my dreams, I thought.

"That might be hard. I live in Florida," he pronounced.

He might as well have said Australia.

"Florida!" I shouted into the phone.

What was Lynn thinking? My heart sank. This would never work. Jeff suggested that we write letters, and I ended the phone call noncommittally. "Yeah, sure, bye."

I hung up the phone and found Lynn in her bedroom, where I berated her for setting me up with a guy who lived a thousand miles away.

Lynn just kept on smiling. "You two are perfect for each other," she assured me. And then she opened up a photo album from her college days and pointed to a picture of a very cute guy—Jeff.

I stared at a smiling young man. He was handsome. His hair was short and dirty blond, his eyes were green, and he had a beautiful smile. She showed me other pictures and told me that Jeff was in the Navy, in flight school. He wanted to fly F-14s one day. When I saw Jeff in his uniform, my heart melted like butter. He was the most handsome man I had ever seen. Maybe a thousand miles away wasn't so bad.

Soon thereafter, Jeff and I started speaking by telephone, and I received his first letter. We had a lot in common. I read his letter over and over. He sounded too good to be true. Every time the phone rang, my heart would jump into my head. Some days I paced in my driveway impatiently for the mailman. With every phone call, my feelings grew deeper. With every letter, I knew he was the one.

One night, just two months after we had our first conversation, it happened. Jeff called late in the night. He was so worried about a flight he had the next day that he couldn't get to sleep. He told me about his tests and how hard they were. I tried to comfort him the best I could, but I didn't really know what to say since I knew nothing about flying. Our conversation was going nowhere. He decided to hang up and get some sleep.

After he said bye, I paused and said, "I love you." Where those words came from I'm not sure. They popped out of my mouth before I could stop them. I panicked and swallowed hard. There was a long pause. I knew I had blown it with him. Never tell a man you've never met that you love him! I closed my eyes to hold back the tears and waited for him to say something.

"I love you, too," Jeff replied. "What are we going to do about it?" he asked.

"Guess we have to meet," I suggested, with tears of joy rolling down my cheeks. It was early November, and Jeff told me he would be coming home to New York for Christmas break. Instead of heading straight home, he would make a pit stop in Boston.

Jeff and I met a week before Christmas. It was wonderful. We connected instantly and got along so well that I went with him to New York to meet his family that same week. His parents were a bit shocked, but we all got along so well, we all forgot that Jeff and I had only just officially met days before.

Two months later, I traveled to Florida and saw where he lived and worked.

It was an exciting time. Fighter jets; sunshine; white, sandy beaches; and Jeff in a uniform made my head spin and my heart throb. It was like living in the movie *Top Gun*.

A month later, I said goodbye to my best friend, Lynn, who tried really hard not to shout, "I told you so!" That's okay; it was the best "I told you so" of my life.

I moved to Florida and set up house in a small apartment. A month after that, we were engaged; two months later we were married. A year later, Jeff was flying F-14s, and soon we were living in Japan and traveling the world.

Much of our marriage has been spent in separation because of the Navy lifestyle. We have hundreds of letters that we've written to each other over the years. In fact, I think the first eight years of our marriage could be told in detail just by reading our letters. But it was those letters in the beginning that taught us the most about each other. We fell in love with each other based on who we were, not what we looked like or what we could do for the other person. It wasn't love at first sight. It was love at first read.

—JENNIFER B. REED

Jennifer and Jeff celebrated their 10-year wedding anniversary in June (and October) 2000. They secretly married in Florida, then had a garden wedding at Jennifer's parents' home in Massachusetts a few months later. They never believed in doing things the conventional way. Now they live in Maryland with their two children, leading a somewhat normal life, but are always open for the unexpected.

A Gift for Daddy

My husband, Danny, and I were married in 1990. I was 18, he was 24. I married him with the knowledge that he had been a juvenile diabetic since the age of 10. Nevertheless, we said our vows "in sickness and in health, for richer or poorer, in good times and bad, till death do us part." We were very much in love and prepared to take whatever life threw our way.

Two years after we were married, Danny went legally blind from the complications of diabetes. They saved a little sight in one eye, but nothing in the other. As devastated as we were, life went on. We focused on our dreams of having a child together.

Two years later, I was still not pregnant, and we received the bad news that Danny's kidneys were failing, and he would soon need kidney dialysis. We took a deep breath and went on with plans to buy our first home, still wishing for the child we wanted so badly.

There were numerous hospitalizations for infections and other complications due to the diabetes over the next two years. I watched the man I loved so much go slowly downhill. One night we discussed the subject of trying one more time for a child. We were well aware of the risks involved to a child born of a diabetic and that the chances of conception at this point were far below the norm. Still, we decided to try once more.

We hadn't tried in several years, having resolved ourselves to the fact that we would be childless.

We armed ourselves with fertility education and an ovulation predictor kit, and we waited for my ovulation time to begin. To us, it seemed like an eternity to wait for a month, but in reality, we had been waiting six years.

On Valentine's Day, 1996, we found out I was pregnant. We were ecstatic at the realization that our dream would come true. Despite what we had gone through and would go through in the unforeseen future, we were so grateful for the gift that we were about to receive.

My pregnancy went well until the sixth month, when, ironically, I was diagnosed as a gestational diabetic. We were scared to death. It was controlled with diet, and I was required to check my blood sugar every day. It gave me greater empathy for what my husband had to endure, although at least I didn't have to take insulin.

Our beautiful son, Devin James, was born October 19, 1996. He was born into a joyous family that knew the ache of not conceiving. Danny was a proud papa. He was also my lifesaver. Devin wasn't too interested in breastfeeding or sleeping. It was Danny who stayed up with him, often falling asleep with him in his arms. It was

Danny, who with the assistance of his mom, stayed home with him so I could be the breadwinner.

Danny and Devin formed a bond that was unbreakable. Life was good for a while and we marveled at this perfect, healthy little miracle whom we cradled in our arms and thanked God for.

The year 1998 started out good. It had been two full years since any major medical complications, when Danny was hospitalized for a double knee replacement because his knees had deteriorated due to his kidney failure.

He wanted the knee replacement so he could walk with his son. We celebrated Devin's first birthday in October and the winter brought a few short hospitalizations, but we were making it.

In July of 1998, Danny was hospitalized with a gangrenous toe. Further tests showed that he was losing circulation in both legs below the knees. They tried to save his right leg with a vein graft but had to amputate the day after his thirty-third birthday.

Danny and I had long conversations about Devin. This was a man whom I'd never seen break down. He was now almost always on the verge of tears. He'd been in the hospital for a month already, and now his other leg was deteriorating. He wanted to give up. He worried that Devin's friends would think of him as a freak and that he'd no longer be able to do the things with him that he'd done previously. I told him that no matter what happened, he was the same person that Devin knew and loved. Devin was Daddy's boy.

A week after they amputated his right leg, emergency surgery was performed to remove Danny's gangrenous colon. He was in intensive care when the doctor explained that his EKG had changed. It was at this point that I became very scared of losing Danny.

I didn't speak to him about it because I knew how fragile he was. I just kept reminding him that he had a little boy at home who needed him and that he had to fight. Devin's second birthday was coming up, and Danny wanted to be home for it. In reality, I was coming to terms with the fact that everything seemed to be going wrong and that Danny's body was suffering the end result of brittle diabetics. I started grieving that Danny would not be around to see Devin go to his first day of school, go on his first date, and so on.

Danny's other leg was amputated two weeks later. He came home to us right before Devin's second birthday. We celebrated, family and friends, the second birthday of our miracle child and Danny's homecoming. He'd been away for three months.

After the party, I noticed a change in Danny. He seemed withdrawn. He went to bed extremely early every night. It seemed to me as if the birthday party was his climax, and now he was too tired to go on. He lost so much weight you could see his heart beating in his chest. Danny told me that he was okay, but I knew that he wasn't.

Devin shared his bedroom with Danny. Five days after Devin's second birthday, on October 24, 1998, Devin climbed out of his crib for the first time. I grabbed Devin before he woke up Daddy and then talked on the phone to my mom for an hour. I wanted to let Danny sleep in. I went to wake him to tell him that we had to get ready to go to dialysis. His eyes were closed, and he had a slight smile on his face. I could not wake up my Danny. On this day, at the age of 26, I became a widow.

Devin didn't understand—he thought that Daddy was just sleeping. It has now been two years since Danny's passing, and I still don't think Devin understands. We have told him that his Daddy is in heaven, in the sky, and we have regularly visited the cemetery, where our last family picture is on the tombstone. Devin stopped talking about his daddy, so I figured he'd forgotten him.

Then one day, a short while ago, Devin and I were shopping in Wal-Mart. I asked Devin if he wanted to give Daddy something at his grave. He pointed to a heart balloon that said "I Love You." The perfect gift—it was exactly four years after we found out that we were pregnant on Valentine's Day! I grabbed it, figuring that when we got to the cemetery, he would decide that he wanted to take it home. We got in the car, and all of a sudden Devin said that he wanted to let the balloon go up to Daddy up in heaven. I was awestruck by his comment since he hadn't spoken of him in a long time.

When we got to the gravesite, the skies were cloudy and a storm was brewing. I asked him if he was sure he wanted to let the balloon go, and he said yes. I took the weight off of the balloon, and a wind gust knocked it to the ground. Devin started crying, saying it wouldn't get to Daddy.

Just then the balloon rose into the sky. The higher it went, the more excited Devin became. Soon it was out of our sight. He asked me if I thought Daddy got his balloon. I smiled through my tears and said, "Yes baby, he did, and he's smiling down right now on his little boy he still loves."

As I watch Devin grow, I will always remind him of the daddy who loved him and helped bring him into the world. And when he is too old to remember, I will also tell him the story about a little boy who loved his daddy so much, he sent an "I love you" balloon up to heaven.

I will give him a copy of this book when he is old enough to treasure it, and he will read of the love his daddy had for him, always. And he will know that his daddy's love for him knew no bounds. He was, and still is, Daddy's boy.

—CINDY A. DONIGIAN

Cindy and Devin live in the same house they did two years ago. Cindy enjoys taking care of her Great Dane, St. Bernard, and cocker spaniel, and Devin. Devin goes to preschool and loves collecting bugs and frogs. They have a new person in their life who has asked to adopt Devin and has proposed to Cindy. She hasn't given an answer yet, but thinks she may say yes . . .

Mirror Image

MY SIX-YEAR-OLD DAUGHTER, SARAH, IS THE SPITTING IMAGE OF ME. Her thick wavy brown hair and brown eyes with a slight oriental shape to them look identical to baby pictures of me from that same age. She's a cuddly, robust, sunny child with a pudgy belly, portraying her love for sweets and enthusiasm about eating, and her genetic disposition toward overweight.

From the moment she was born, family has commented on the resemblance between Sarah and me. As she grows older, she only looks more and more like her mama. Gazing at my daughter is like looking into a mirror that allows me to peek into my childhood.

My four-and-a-half-year-old daughter, Elana, looks like she was either adopted or born from an illicit affair with a man other than her daddy. Trust me, she's ours. But with fine blond hair and striking blue eyes, as hard as I have tried, I have been unable to come up with one single physical resemblance between she and me.

The only way we are sure that she came from me is witnessing the birth process I went through to bring her into this world. She was not switched at birth in the hospital, we are reassured. If you look really, really hard, you might see a bit of grandpa's eyes in hers, and the shape of her face somewhat resembles her daddy's. Somewhat—it's a bit of a stretch. Elana will tell you, "I don't look like anyone in my family!"

Elana and Sarah are inseparable sisters, connected at the hip, and constantly playing or fighting with one another. Never fails, when people meet them for the first time, they pause, look them over carefully, and declare, "My goodness, they look nothing like one another."

Yes, it's true, my daughters are as different as night and day. The ways that Elana differs from her mama extend beyond her physical appearance. Whereas my mother reports that I was an even-tempered, happy baby, and my disposition these days is rather steady and calm, Elana breaks into hysteria and wails of whining at the first hint of a disappointment. She is easily upset and a temperamental, moody child. Elana also has the greatest laugh I've ever heard when her daddy tickles her. The same child's spirit that easily descends into despair when she doesn't get her way also rises like a helium balloon when she has a tickle session with her daddy, or gets hold of one of her favorite foods, or is engaged in play with her beloved sister or a favored babysitter.

The differences between Elana and her sister, and between Elana and me, are an incredible blessing, and this is exactly how it is meant to be. Sisters so close in age are natural competitors. If Elana were beautiful in the same way as Sarah, others would always be comparing them, with one of them winning the "most beautiful" category.

Now, it is impossible to declare which of my beauties wins the contest. They are both gorgeous in completely different ways. Do you prefer the looks of the stunning, take-your-breath-away radiance of a dark-haired little girl, or the angelic loveliness of a wisp of a child who looks at you with her baby blues and melts your heart?

Which one of my little girls is the smarter one, or the tougher one, or the most clever? Each in her own way demonstrates those qualities as much as the other, just differently. Sibling rivalry is ever present in our household, especially when it comes to competing for the affection of their mama, but I don't worry at all about the girls being compared to one another, with one always feeling the lesser in comparison to the other.

The girls have the opportunity to be close sisters, yet entirely individuals—something that would have been much more difficult if they were the spitting image of each other.

I have also come to see another blessing in Elana's unique appearance and personality. When I gaze into Elana's face, it might not appear as if I am looking in a looking glass, but she mirrors me in many, not as obvious, ways. Elana plays out the temperamental nature I would probably display if I were not so controlled and self-disciplined. Elana giggles like I wish I could if I could relax my self-consciousness. Elana loves to play, something that I don't take the time for much anymore. Elana mirrors aspects of the girl I wish I could be, if I were able to take off the adult mask and just be myself.

I say, "just be myself," even though, apparently, there's little about Elana that is just like myself. That is only true at a surface level. Elana is very much her mother's daughter. She and I share a secret, one she is too young now to appreciate.

If her mama could relax and give up all pretenses of being the perfect mother, wife, and daughter, she would probably act in the world a whole lot like Elana. Elana is my mirror image, reflecting aspects of me that are undeveloped, hidden from view, or secondary to my primary nature. She completes me, instead of just reflecting me.

As for the blond hair and blue eyes, I figure God placed her in such a body so that she and I could keep this revelation a secret. That way, when she's acting out in a less-than-pleasing manner, I can detach from the scene and say, with amazement, "This is my daughter? Where did she come from?"

—AZRIELA JAFFE

Elana, her sister Sarah, and her brother Elijah continue to be, in their mama's eyes, three of the most beautiful, charming, loving, and fantastic kids in the universe. Yes, mama is a bit biased, but really, it's true. When mama isn't taking care of her kids, she's writing books and her syndicated newspaper column, "Advice from A-Z," where she advises self-employed professionals and employees on work and family concerns.

$\mathcal{D}$ancing in the Aisles

Money was a precious commodity and time together even more scarce in the early years of our marriage of almost two decades.

My husband, Michael, and I juggled opposite work schedules and shared household duties, savoring one another's company in the still hours of the night when the world became our own private playground.

While most people were settling in for the night, we were eagerly venturing from our modest three-room apartment to gather treasured memories of playing hilarious matches of tennis in the dark; taking long, contemplative walks under the glow of streetlights; swimming lazily under twinkling stars; or competing in friendly rounds of miniature golf at a nearby twenty-four-hour course.

Our wonderful, spontaneous excursions took the sting out of the endless hours we spent apart.

Although we discovered many creative and inexpensive ways to enjoy our limited time together, there was one place we returned to again and again.

By far, our most cherished date was dancing in the aisles of the supermarket.

On many evenings, long after midnight and in the calm of an all-night grocery store, we would sway gracefully to the melodies flowing from the overhead Muzak that filled the empty aisles. Oblivious to other nocturnal shoppers and store personnel, we sashayed down one lane and up another in a tender and playful embrace, filling our shopping cart with necessities and our hearts with romance.

It was in those innocent days of twirling among the cabbages and oranges, the boxes of Jell-O and cartons of milk, that we unwittingly defined our relationship and set the tone for our future together. Amid pot roasts and canned vegetables, we learned to mingle the mundane with the eternal, accepting our challenges and successes while staying focused on each other and the love that brought us together in the first place. Surrounded by bags of chips and sponge mops, we became best friends, ready to respond to life's triumphs and tragedies.

Adversity inevitably finds its way to every home, and we have been no exception. In our modest seventeen years of marriage, we have experienced many things most couples will avoid throughout a lifetime. We have suffered the discouragement of infertility, the worry of illness, and the loneliness of rejection. We have endured the fearful frustration of unemployment, the weariness of unexpected debt, and the agony of losing precious loved ones to miscarriage and stillbirths.

While every couple must find its own way to face the difficult times while protecting the romance, for us, the answer for hanging in there through the hard times has always been a simple one. We have never stopped dancing in the aisles. Almost every time we have gone to the store together, in good times and in bad, in sickness and in health, in depression and joy, when we've been madly in love, and when we've been feeling wounded by the other, we have danced together.

We have learned to feel safe with one another while dancing in those aisles. We have learned to trust and to go with the flow, while dancing, and also, in the flow of life. We have learned to make life an adventure and to find joy despite whatever circumstances we may face.

Only one thing has changed about dancing in the supermarket all these years. Now the kids try to cut in, and customers look at us as though we've lost our minds, because when you dance in the aisles at any time other than after midnight, there are lots of people around! But, we've also had our share of customers stop and comment that they can tell we are very much in love and that we enjoy each other's company.

We have learned to count our blessings and prepare for our future. We have marveled at the miracle of birth and the sublime joy of parenting. We understand the power of prayer and righteous living. We are privileged to have shared hopes and dreams. We appreciate these major life experiences all the more because we never forgot how to have fun and laugh a little along the way.

Midnight waltzes have given way to sometimes chaotic Saturday family shopping trips; his hair is now more gray than chestnut colored, and my girlish figure is well padded. Money remains a precious commodity, and time alone together is scarcer than ever.

Hand-in-hand, we continue to dance the dance of daily life with the same beauty and enthusiasm and love as in those days of sweet innocence. Or, maybe, even more so. You see, we have come to understand the wisdom that longtime dance partners already know. The longer you dance together, the better it is.

—AMANDA KRUG

Amanda and Michael are the proud and busy parents of four amazing and "perfect-for-us" children— Abby, Lilli, Evan, and Grant. They live in Fishers, Indiana, located in the heart of their beloved Hoosier homeland. Amanda is a full-time homemaker (the best job in the world, she says); Michael works for a local strategic and e-business consulting firm. They believe their marriage was handpicked by Heavenly Father and thank Him each day for the incredible blessing of sharing their lives together.

Moving Day

THE DAY STARTED EARLY. MOVING DAY IS NEVER EASY. SOMEHOW there just doesn't seem to be enough daylight hours to get everything packed, loaded, transported, and delivered.

This was a bittersweet day, indeed. Even though my daughter, Becky, had already moved away from home, she continued to live nearby. She was just a few minutes away, and our endless telephone calls were free.

She dropped by for dinner almost every day.

Becky's desire was to get a degree in criminal justice. There are no local colleges in our area; therefore, she would have to attend college away from home. She chose a college 70 miles away. She liked the atmosphere and the course of study at that particular school, but the thing that had attracted her the most was the fact that it was only an hour away from home. Even though she couldn't drop by every day, as she had been accustomed, she could come home on the weekends.

We had the utilities connected in her apartment. She arranged her class schedule. While she was excited, I could tell right away that she wasn't overly eager to move. That was fine with me, as I knew it would be difficult for me, as well. When my twin sons, Brad and Chad, went off to college several years before, I was very sad. It was even more difficult this time. Becky was my baby. Her excitement and enthusiasm for life kept me feeling young. I wondered how I would cope when she moved away.

My husband, Roy, went to pick up the moving truck. Once he arrived at her house, our sons met him there. They loaded it with boxes full of Becky's treasures. "Taking her posters down was sad," her dad confided in me the next day. "Packing her clothes was even more difficult." After a few hours, her first "home away from home" was empty. Becky shut the door for the final time.

Roy drove the truck, while Becky and her brothers followed in their cars.

I left earlier that day, knowing that I couldn't stand packing up her belongings. When I got to her new apartment, I noticed a tear on her cheek as the men unloaded her things.

I placed my arm around her waist. "Seventy miles is not really that far," I reassured Becky, trying desperately to refrain from crying. "It only takes a little over an hour to get back home." She stood silently. "And you can call us collect anytime that you want to," I further commented. I don't know whom I was trying the hardest to convince that we would survive this event, her or myself.

Busily, we unloaded the truck and stacked boxes in her new living room. Her landlady was nice enough to allow her to keep Sweetie Pie, her kitten. I felt much better leaving Becky with her beloved kitten. I gave her a farewell hug and kiss and quickly left before I cried.

"She has plenty to keep her busy unloading all those boxes," I convinced myself, as I pulled out of her new driveway and headed back down the interstate. When I got back to town, I drove slowly by Becky's first home away from home. A lump came to my throat and I wanted to burst into tears. I realized, however, that she had to grow up, and I was proud that she had decided to go back to college.

When I returned home, Roy was pulling the moving truck onto the driveway.

"Follow me to the gas station to return the truck," he shouted from the open window. We took the truck back, settled the bill, and quietly rode back home together. Neither of us uttered a single word. We were both tired and upset about having to leave Becky that far away from us.

When we returned home, I went to my computer, hoping that it would take my mind off of her absence. Roy went to his study, as well. We both knew what the other was thinking and also knew that we didn't need to discuss the issue at that time. We both had some major adjusting to do.

Suddenly, I heard the back door open. I jumped up from my computer, but before I got to the kitchen, I heard the sweetest voice shout with delight.

"I'm home!" As I met Becky, I saw a big smile on her face. Roy came running into the room, as well.

"You're back?" I exclaimed. "I'm so glad to see you." The three of us were in the kitchen, laughing and hugging, like we hadn't seen each other in a month.

"I missed you both so much," she sheepishly admitted. "As soon as Daddy pulled out of the driveway, I got lonely," she confessed. "Can we watch a movie together?" she inquired, trying to change the subject.

We popped some popcorn, put a movie into the VCR, and settled down in the living room. Together, we watched a portion of the movie. We all fell asleep in front of the TV. I awoke in the middle of the night. I went over to Becky, got her up, gave her a goodnight kiss, and sent her to her old bed. I crawled into my bed and smiled, knowing that my baby was in the room down the hall.

The next day, after some much-needed rest, Becky returned to her new apartment. Classes started a few days later. She is happy there now, and we are happy for her.

Becky continues to come home as often as possible. Her visits never fail to bring joy to our lives. To this day, when she comes home, she always shouts, "I'm home," as she walks through the door.

And she is. This will always be her home.

—NANCY GIBBS

Over the past year, Becky has excelled in her classes. She is excited about her course of study and has decided to work toward a double major—criminal justice and computer science. Nancy and Roy are very proud of her and also of their twin sons, Brad and Chad. Fortunately, all three siblings live in the same town and spend a great deal of time together. And they all still see plenty of Mom and Dad, too!

In Sickness and in Sickness, Till Death Do Us Part

"WE CAN'T TELL ANYBODY ABOUT THIS," SAID MY TALL, BLONDE, handsome husband.

"C'mon, Randy! How about your own mother!" I implored. "Good grief! She lives with us! We can't keep this from her, the kids, or to ourselves. We are going to go crazy!"

My husband had been having unexplained physical problems for a few months.

His arms and legs would get all tingly and go numb. Severe fatigue dominated his days. As assistant fire chief he had an important, physical job that required that he be in top form all the time, around the clock. Several trips to a neurologist as well as two MRIs confirmed the worst.

Multiple sclerosis.

"How can this be? My sister has had the same disease for twenty years," Randy told his doctor. The doctor explained all the unknowns in a generic and unsatisfactory manner because there just aren't answers. It is a mysterious affliction that affects millions of people.

We muddled through the day with our hearts holding each other together. Our individual thoughts and feelings swirled about our heads as if in a wild whirlpool. What about work? Who would take care of our five acres of land? How would we deal with such an unknown future? Where should we go for information? When will our life really change for the worst?

It had been a really hard year already. We had felt the providence of God guiding and protecting us in all our previous trials. He would do so now, we resolved.

That evening, the fire chief paid a visit to our home.

"Randy, I am going to retire and have asked the Board of Directors to appoint you as the official fire chief. Will you accept the position?"

This was too much on the very same day! The Chief must've thought my husband was crazy because he said he'd have to think about it and get back to him the next day. Lest you think this was great timing, because maybe the fire chief job would be less physically demanding for Randy, it was just the opposite. Randy would have 200 square miles, 6 stations, and over 100 people to supervise! It was a big deal.

The next day, he declared that yes, he would be delighted to accept the new responsibility, albeit with fear and trepidation! He was highly respected and loved, and somehow, with the support of those who cared about him, we'd handle this new pressure and opportunity.

Life moved on. Randy's symptoms came and went, multiplied and divided. Luckily he has always been a health nut and an athlete. That kept his body and mind in fine form and remissions more the norm than exacerbations. We feared I might have to care for an invalid, and we emotionally prepared for that.

But adversity sometimes takes uncanny twists.

Randy now cares for me more than I care for him. He never expected his zany, healthy wife to get ill, and neither did I. But shortly after Randy's diagnosis, chronic asthma, diabetes, and ulcerative colitis jumped into my being and surprised us both. Suddenly, I required as much, or sometimes more, medical attention and flexibility as Randy did. We weren't sure anymore who was taking care of whom and "who was the sickest." And it didn't really matter. This wasn't a contest.

Before we became ill, Randy and I did mega entertaining. Our hospitality house was a joy. We loved having folks over for meals or just for fun, chat, and games. The door was revolving with teenagers, missionaries, meetings, and mayhem. Now, such activity has tapered down to a drizzle. We entertain selectively due to Randy's fatigue or my either hacking with asthma, in the bathroom with colitis, or out of whack with low or high blood sugar from diabetes.

But lest you think that Randy and I are bedridden invalids, never leaving the house anymore, you'd be wrong! Sure, we have to plan for all kinds of possible medical emergencies, but on a good day, you'll catch me on the back of our Harley-Davidson, the Dyna Wide Glide! (I used to have my own baby blue and hot pink Honda Spree, but now we share a bike.)

It is hilarious to watch us on the bike together. Randy is slender and very young looking, and I am rather short, round, and matronly (dang!). I have a black leather jacket and a gaudy-as-heck helmet with orange and black flames. Randy's tasteful helmet is just black and silver.

We have great fun riding to church on Sundays!

Our adventurous spirit isn't always in alignment with our bodies. Recently we took a jaunt to Crater Lake, Oregon. It rained, hailed, and thunderstormed, but we were prepared with our rain gear. Unfortunately we had neglected to put spare clothes, medications, and inhalers into waterproof bags, so everything got soggy. I was so tired after so much excitement that, lulled by the *ping, ping* of the rain and hail on my helmet and the swaying of the motorcycle in motion, I fell asleep clinging to Randy on the back of the bike.

As a diabetic, sleep is good, but eating is better. I skipped eating when I was supposed to. When we stopped at a gorgeous park, with the sun finally shining, to stretch our legs, I promptly fell off the bike. By the time we got home I was in bad shape—crying, shaking, in a muddle. Randy fed and took care of me, as he often does.

Many spouses divorce their mates when a dreaded disease is diagnosed. This was never an option and never will be. Ruth Graham, Billy Graham's wife, has been known to say, "Murder, maybe. Divorce? Never!" You might think that all of our various ailments have killed us in the romance and sex department. Thank God, it's just the opposite. Since both of us became ill, romance and physical intimacy have become dearer.

When faced with the possibility of our own mortality, it became easier to sweep away all the small stuff of life and the nuisances that crop up in every marriage. Instead, now we focus more easily on our love and commitment to each other.

Randy and I have both become weaker in body but stronger in how we value our lives and each other. The passion is stronger than ever between us, even if the bodies are not always as willing. After being together for 30 years, we have discovered a perfect way of loving that transcends illnesses or quirky behavior, and a caring that continually changes and grows no matter what adversity life throws our way.

It's called love.

—PATTI IVERSON

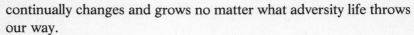 *Patti Iverson lives in Medford, Oregon, with her fire chief. They jaunt about the country (when able) on their Harley-Davidson. Patti occasionally dresses up in her clown outfit and provides cheer when the situation warrants it or the price is right. Both are actively involved in church, community, family, and friends.*

Friends for 43 Years

I MET MAE FORD IN 1957, A FEW DAYS AFTER MY MAMA AND I MOVED from our home in Hampton, Virginia, to the country, and I do mean country, in Newland, North Carolina. Gramma and Grampa were getting too old to care for themselves, and my mama, being the only widow among the sisters, was expected to pick up all of her belongings and move back home to care for her parents.

No, they didn't ask for my opinion. I was a lowly teenager going into the tenth grade. My grandfather really did not want me to come at all. I still have the letter he wrote, telling my mother that she could send me to Crossnore and I could get a good education there, that they were old and a teenager would be hard for them to put up with.

The Crossnore home was an orphanage. Mama replied quickly with a "NO!" If I wasn't welcome, then she would not come. Good for her. I guess he backed down, because we did move.

I tried to make the best of it, and now I realize that it was the best thing that ever happened to me. Because I met my best friend ever.

I met Mae working as a waitress at my brother's restaurant, where I also worked. We both clicked right off, and we made each working day a lot of fun. It was hard work, too. We started early and stayed late, taking a break when my brother, Earl, would go home for a rest after the lunch crowd.

Mae and I would grab a grapette and a bag of chips, sit down by the window, and act like we owned the place. I would boss the young dishwasher around and tell her I could fire her because my brother owned the place.

I made a big mistake one day and did fire her, and when Earl came back from his little nap, he made me go wash dishes. Mae came to my rescue and helped me. We were both so mad and you would think I would have learned something, but I didn't. I kept my big mouth going, and it is still going strong. Mae would attest to that.

Mae was a basketball star—she could rack up more baskets than anyone I had ever seen. I did not have an athletic bone in my body, but I have a big mouth, so I made the cheerleader team so that I could go to all the games with Mae. I would cheer like crazy for her, and she would continue to rack up the points.

Mae lived out of town in a small community called Cow Camp. I loved it out there at her house. Her dad had a small dairy and lots of cows, and Mae had to call the cows in each evening. This was a job to Mae but fun and adventure for me. Mae would make funny noises calling the cows into the barn from up in the mountain and down they would come. She would holler, "Nanci, get out of the way, now, here they come." I would run like the wind so that they could get through the narrow gate and head down to the barn.

Lordy, I was a city girl. I thought someone made milk in jars; I had no idea those big-eyed animals had anything to do with it.

I made quite a name for myself that fall in school as a fast city girl, which of course I was not. I figured what the heck, who cared how I behaved, even though I knew I was an honor roll student. I thought Mama was too busy caring for her parents to worry about me. Little did I know Mama's health was slipping from such hard work, and by January of 1958 I got the devastating news that we were moving back home to Virginia.

Now that may sound strange that I was upset, but I had fallen in love with that country town and many of the people, and of course, Mae. The morning we moved, Mae walked all the way from Cow Camp to say goodbye. We were trying very hard to be brave and to keep laughing. I started singing "Carry Me Back to Old Virginny" at the top of my lungs, and Mae was trying to drown me out with "Nothing Could Be Finer Than to Be in Carolina in the Morning." We were a pitiful sight. I cried all 500 miles back home.

At my new school, despite my grief, it didn't take me long to get back in the groove. I started going steady with a boy named Doug and spent the school year dancing at school dances and having a ball swimming and sunning at the beach with all my friends. I was selected for a capella choir, and Mama was able to scrape together sixteen dollars so that I could go to music camp that summer.

Then tragedy struck on June 16, 1959, when my dear brother Paul died after a long illness. He and his devoted wife, Ruth, always looked out for Mama and me, and I knew Mama was going to miss this special son of hers. My older brothers decided for us that we were moving to Louisiana, where my oldest brother lived, so that he could watch over us.

I had one year left of school, and I fussed and cried about moving to Shreveport, Louisiana. It was a big change from Hampton, and an even bigger change than Newland. It was a big city, and it was so hot that shacks along the roadside had air conditioners, and children never played outside.

I was angry at being uprooted again. My poor mother was in shock over losing her thirty-three-year-old son. I was being separated from my longtime boyfriend, my high school, my friends. Finally, after much complaining, I got permission from my mother to move back to Hampton just for the summer, to live with my brother Tom and his family.

Oh, I was so happy to get back. I hadn't been gone for a month, but it seemed like years and time just flew by. When it was time to head back to Louisiana and enter my senior year, I was torn between leaving my boyfriend, Doug, and going back to my mother. Doug wanted me to stay and get married. I agreed. My mother allowed it, as long as I finished high school.

We had to go to Elizabeth City, North Carolina, to get married because I was underage (only 17) and such weddings were prohibited in Virginia. We lived with Doug's wonderful parents during my last year of high school.

I wrote my longtime friend Mae after the fact and told her we were married. Her mother, Rachel, received the letter and sent it to her. She had married an airman stationed at Langley Air Force Base, and—what a wonderful coincidence—she lived just a couple of miles from us. In fact, my husband, Doug, worked at NASA, located on Langley Air Force Base.

Mae had no idea she was anywhere near me. As soon as she got my letter, we were on the phone. Doug and I drove to Grafton to find them. I will never forget that day. We jumped and hugged each other like little children. I met her husband, Pat, and he was dressed all in black, so good looking. I remember telling her he looked like Zorro. Pat was a lot like Doug, very quiet and a little shy, but once you got to know him, you could tell he was a nice guy. He and Mae were very happy.

They didn't have much, and neither did we. We spent as much time together as possible. With me being in school so much, weekends we were always together. Soon Mae was pregnant with her son Tommy, and we walked a lot, picking up empty drink bottles and carrying them back to the store to exchange for the deposit money on the bottles. We would buy whatever we could, sometimes a hotdog or one can of sauerkraut, which we would carry back to her place and share. She had a thing for sauerkraut when she was pregnant.

When her oil was all gone and there was no heat, we just kept our coats on.

Many times my father-in-law would come to pick me up and tell Mae to get her things and come with us. When Pat traveled, she'd live with us, treated like family.

Her son Tommy was born in July of 1960, and our daughter Sherry was born in December of 1960. We raised our children together. When their home was destroyed by a northeaster, they moved in with us until they could get settled again elsewhere. In 1963, when Pat was discharged from the Air Force, they moved back home to North Carolina.

Our friendship has remained strong throughout all these years. Mae went to work at a hosiery mill in Newland and gave me my very first pair of panty hose. We laughed and laughed about me putting my plump fanny into that very small looking wad of panty hose. But they stretched (a lot) and I loved them. Our children grew up to be good friends, more like brothers and sisters.

Mae and Pat would have celebrated their fortieth wedding anniversary in May of 1998 but Pat didn't make it. Right before Easter that year, Pat suffered a massive coronary and died in Mae's arms. He had only another week until retirement from his job. It was a tragic loss.

I had breast cancer in 1986 and my prognosis was very poor. Mae and I decided we'd better make the most of our remaining time together, like we've always done. We are practically inseparable, even though we live apart.

My friendship with Mae is as solid as the Grandfather Mountain. Mama always told me if you can look back on your life and you have had one friend who has stuck with you through thick and thin, who doesn't bad-mouth you, who cares for you no matter what, then you are blessed.

I am blessed by my lifelong friend, Mae.

—NANCI L. STROUPE

Mae has proven herself a survivor, working full-time and spending most of her free time with her only grandchild, Rachel, and Rachel's parents, Tommy and

Keila. She also lovingly cares for her own mother, Rachel, who is 93 years old.

Nanci is still going strong and in remission now for the past 14 years, enjoying all four of her grandchildren: Ashley, Emily, Angelina, and Dustin. Learning at a young age that life is so fragile, she and her husband of 40 years enjoy and appreciate their life, knowing that each day is a gift from God and taking it one day at a time.

$\mathcal{A}$ Jewel in My Crown

I WAS 23 YEARS OLD, PREGNANT, AND EXPERIENCING MORNING SICKNESS from one morning until the next. I was a relatively new nurse and was in charge of B wing of a large nursing home. I have always loved children and the elderly. I thought it was the perfect job—until I met Mr. Elam. I dreaded going into his room, more than that of anyone else. He was the grouchiest person I'd ever met. He never had a kind word for anyone or anything, including me.

I had to give Mr. Elam feedings in his stomach tube twice on my shift. This was 23 years ago, and they were made with something that smelled so foul that I would try to hold my breath during the whole procedure. He would prolong the whole ordeal by holding his stomach muscles, and that would delay the feeding's going in. I would have to leave the room for a short while because it sickened me so, which seemed to delight him.

Oh yes, he was one mean fellow.

One day he absolutely drew on my last nerve, and I exclaimed to him, "Mr. Elam, you need to thank *God* that you have your mind and you're able to think for yourself!"

He responded boldly with, "What God? There is no *God!*"

I can tell you, those words scared me to death! I had never heard anyone really say that and mean it. I was definitely naïve . . . but I was afraid lightning was going to strike him from the heavens . . . and I'd be sitting way too close!

Subconsciously, I made that man my mission. I had no idea how I was going to do it, but I had to make sure he *knew* there was a *God!*

Mr. Elam was not bed confined, but he refused to get out of bed. The nurses' aides and I would turn him about 20 times in an eight-hour shift to keep him from getting bed sores, and less than one minute later he would roll back onto his back. Did I mention he was stubborn?

I started going into work an hour early and taking cards and games with me. I would play rummy with him and talk about God. We'd play Scrabble, and I'd talk about all my blessings. He eventually opened up with some information that alluded to his mean-spiritedness. He was a successful engineer and designed many tools for the space program. He had lost his wife of 42 years a few months before he lost his stomach to cancer. Since he had no stomach, he could not swallow a single bite of food. I think that's when I first softened up to him—I could not imagine my life without food.

I knew he looked forward to my visits every day before my shift, because he actually got mad when I didn't make it to his room one day when I had a prenatal visit and was late for work. He ignored me completely and held up his tube feeding even longer that day. I was very aware he was mad at me!

I kept trying to tease him and he finally yelled, "I thought you had been in an accident when you didn't show up today! Could you let me know when you're not coming!"

I apologized and couldn't keep from smiling. It was then that I knew that my visits were making a difference.

Mr. Elam had an adopted daughter, so he had never been around a pregnant woman. When the baby started kicking, I asked him if he'd like to feel the kicks. He very timidly touched my stomach and was astounded. Of course, I delighted in telling him that only God could create something so precious.

Then one day he asked me bluntly, "Sue, why is it so important to you that I believe in God?"

I told him that my Granny Baker had told me that for every soul you helped save, God puts a jewel in your crown. I told him I figured if I helped him find the Lord, I'd have the biggest jewel in heaven. We both laughed.

I started bringing my Bible with me, and he would quote the words as I read. That astonished me. I asked him, "If you know this Bible inside out, how can you not believe in God?" He said they were nothing but words . . . just words.

But, I never let up!

My daughter, Shanna Lynn, was born on January 1, 1979. Mr. Elam had spent the last seven months of my pregnancy with me. The weather was so bad that I couldn't get out of the house with her for a month. I had been keeping in touch with the nursing home, and the other nurses told me that Mr. Elam had been asking frequently about Shanna and me. They kept me up on all the news of all the patients, but especially the one who had become my favorite, Mr. Elam.

One day I got the call I had been dreading. Mr. Elam had a blood infection and had been moved to an isolated room. He wasn't expected to live much longer. I knew what I had to do, bad weather or not.

I wrapped up my precious baby girl, trekked over to the nursing home, and took her straight to his room. He was asleep but I nudged him, and when he opened his eyes, I showed him my bundle of joy. He rejoiced with me but was very scared. He told me he had an infection and didn't want her to get ill. "She's lovely, but please take her out. I couldn't stand it if she got sick!" he implored me.

Bless his heart . . . the old grouch really was a loving man. This old man who had made sure I'd thrown up at least three or four more times than necessary every day really had a heart down deep. This old coot had helped me fill my afternoons when my husband worked another shift. He'd filled a big void for me. I'd grown to love this mean old grouch.

My heart was torn. I didn't want him to suffer, but I had hoped in some small way that my daughter could be a surrogate grand-baby for him and maybe give him a reason to live. I took my daughter out to the nurses' station, and they were more than happy to watch her. I went back into Mr. Elam's room and took his hand. He told me that he was going to die soon, and I relayed to him what a privilege it was to take care of him. We laughed and joked about what a difficult patient he had been in the beginning, and he thanked me for making him laugh again.

We could hear my baby screaming, so I reluctantly had to go. I kissed him on the forehead and told him I'd be back to see him. He said, "No, you take care of that baby, I'll see you again."

The baby was now heard all over town, and in the chaos I didn't really catch *exactly* what he had said. I replied, "I know . . . I'll be back!"

He shook his head, smiled, and replied, "I'll find you the next time we see each other! I'll just look for the brightest jewel in heaven . . ."

Mr. Elam died that night.

—SUE HENLEY

Sue Henley has been a nurse for over 26 years, no job harder than the one she had at that nursing home. But she is ever grateful for the experience, and for the love she shared with Mr. Elam. Her daughter Shanna is now 22 years old and married. She has the same generous and God-loving soul as her mother. She teaches special education students, and she and her husband run a camp every summer for the handicapped. Shanna shares her mom with a 13-year-old sister named Tiffany. Shanna and Tiffany are the jewels in Sue's crown.

Sue and her husband, Leonard, have enjoyed marriage for 24 years. She counts her blessings that her family allows her to share so much of herself with her patients.

$\mathcal{T}$he Tarheel and the Spitfire

ANGER IS NOT ONE OF THE EMOTIONS YOU EXPECT TO FEEL WHEN someone proposes marriage to you. But there I was, furious.

"You're mad at me! How can you be mad at me for wanting to marry you?" Mike asked. "You've known me for fourteen years. We have a wonderful time together. We share so much, and you can't deny that something has finally happened to us these past few days." Mike's wrinkled brow illustrated his frustration.

I replied, "I'm not mad at you; I'm mad at the timing. I'm confused, I had my whole life planned out and under control and now . . ."

My voice trailed off, my thoughts evaporating like the little pools of rain at our feet in the hot Florida sun.

"Those plans didn't include falling in love. So what?" Mike responded.

We were at Epcot Center at Disney World, sharing a four-day vacation with my brother Todd and one of my friends from Poland,

Leszek. With two chaperons and a crowded tourist schedule, who would have thought that two old friends would fall truly, madly, deeply in love?

Mike had always had a little crush on me, but I figured that was long over. I was no longer the cute, curvy coed he had met 14 years ago. Besides, he had given up on finding a wife and was really enjoying his bachelorhood. Although he had never settled down with anyone, I had scarcely survived a very bad marriage and a couple of disastrous long-term relationships. These experiences combined with a renewed spiritual relationship had convinced me that life was much safer and saner without men.

"God and me, that's all the relationship I need," I had assured myself. Who needs all the complications that life with a man brings?

This latest complication began when I picked Mike up at the Atlanta airport. He was living in North Carolina and was flying into Atlanta in order to drive down to Orlando with Leszek and myself. It was cheaper to do it this way, and it would give him a chance to get to know Leszek.

Although Mike and I had kept in touch as friends, I had not seen him in a few years. When he came down the hallway from his plane, my heart did the strangest little flip-flop.

"Calm down," I told myself. "This is just Mike, for Pete's sake!"

In the car, I let Mike and Leszek do all the talking, which must have struck them both as pretty strange, since I am such a chatterbox. It was so disconcerting to me to have these strange feelings about Mike, but soon I talked myself out of my reaction. Mike was my dearest, most wonderful friend. I was just happy to finally see him again, I reassured myself.

Besides, in just a few short weeks I would be leaving for Mainland China. A contract waited for my signature at the University in Beijing. I was going to teach there for two years. This trip to Disney World was my last hurrah before I left, and a chance to treat Leszek to Disney World before he went back to Poland. Leszek had been in America for almost a year on a visa. We had met in Poland the year before when he had served as an interpreter for our tour group. He had been all over the United States, but he desperately wanted to meet Donald Duck—an Easter hero in his country—before he returned to Poland.

My brother Todd worked for Disney and was able to get us discounted tickets. Todd had not had some time off in awhile, and so he joined us, giving us an insider's view. It had been a wonderful trip! We were all totally ourselves, having a good time and really enjoying life.

Then, one day, in line for a supersonic hamburger in Tomorrow Land, Mike kissed me on the back of the neck. A soft, tender kiss just below where my ponytail caressed my hairline.

The rest of the day was a blur. I can't even remember where we went, what we ate, or what we did. All I could see, all I could smell, all I noticed was Mike. Were his hands always so graceful? The fingers so long and slender, yet so strong? Were his eyes always that soft sable brown? Did they always have tiny gold flecks? Did his voice always pour out smooth and silky like Tupelo honey? When did that soft Carolina accent become so sexy? How, in 14 years, had I resisted nuzzling a neck that smelled so incredible?

Again, I was uncharacteristically quiet all the way back to Atlanta. Mike had several hours before his flight left, so we drove Leszek to the home where he was staying. Then we went back to my apartment, and I fixed us a bite to eat.

"Well, the first thing I've got to do when I get back to Raleigh is find us a bigger place," he announced. "You still have a lot of stuff," Mike commented. "It's a good thing you didn't get rid of everything like you planned because of China. We'll need most of what you have left."

I sat there on the sofa, looking at him sitting in my favorite overstuffed chair. He was petting my cat, looking perfectly at home. Suddenly, I wasn't angry anymore. Scared to death, perhaps, still stunned, but not angry. Never had something so unexpected felt so absolutely right.

Mike and I set the wedding date for eight months later. No, I never did sign that contract and head over to China. We decided to begin our marriage in Mike's hometown of Raleigh, North Carolina, after two years of living elsewhere in the Tarheel State.

As in any marriage, our love for each other was tested during tumultuous times. While in Raleigh those two years, I was severely injured in a car accident caused by an uninsured driver. Not only would I never live another day totally without pain, but it placed us deeply in debt. Mike was laid off just days before the accident. That might have seemed like a double shot of bad news, but I needed round-the-clock home nursing care, and Mike was there to literally nurse me back to health. If it were possible, we fell deeper in love than before the accident. Just a few days after I was back on my feet, he found another job.

Then four years into our marriage, Mike fell ill. For three months his life hung in the balance, and it was my turn to care for him. Ironically, I was laid off just after he became ill. The doctors at first thought lung cancer was eating away at an artery in his lung, but it turned out the culprit was some strange kind of fungus inhabiting his lung. Part of his lung was surgically removed and, praise God, Mike is in great health today.

While I wouldn't recommend that every married couple go through all the crises we have endured, our relationship has strengthened and deepened as a result. We both know that the other one won't turn and run when the hard times come. We have hundreds of tender memories that keep our love sweet and warm.

One memory in particular never fails to bring a tear to my eye. After Mike's recovery from his lung surgery, he spent many hours pondering why God had saved him in such a miraculous way. Several doctors had told me that first night in the hospital that he would not make it through the night and to call his family. "Why am I here? What plan does God have for my life?" he asked God over and over.

Then one night we lay in bed after saying our prayers and Mike said to me, "I think my purpose in life is to love you. And if that's the only purpose God gives me, that's enough." He found peace that night, and I found another reason to love him and to love the God who brought this wonderful man to my side.

The spring following our wedding, we were both glued to the TV, watching the protests in China and the tanks rolling in. Mike turned to me and teased, "See what I saved you from! Knowing what a spitfire you are, you would have been the first greasy spot under a tank!"

It has been 10 years since we watched those tanks roll. This August will mark the twenty-fifth anniversary of our meeting back at college and the eleventh anniversary of our wedding. Our marriage has seen both of us literally at death's door and close to bankruptcy. We've been to more funerals than weddings and were dealt a blow when we learned we couldn't have children of our own. We've both endured intense physical pain and extreme emotional losses. But we have done it together, the chatterbox spitfire he nick-named "Buckshot" and the soft-spoken Carolina boy with the graceful hands.

Friends first, lovers later, companions for eternity.

—CHERYL NORWOOD

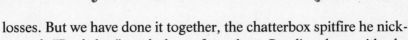 *Cheryl and Mike live in a small suburb of Atlanta with their Siamese cat, Princess Jasmine Poopalot (the "t" is silent, please!). Cheryl is a legal secretary for an Atlanta law firm and Mike sells parts for a Lincoln Mercury dealership. Both are active at Cobb Vinyard Christian Fellowship in Kennesaw, Georgia, and recently celebrated their eleventh wedding anniversary by going to Tours, France! Cheryl won the trip on the Internet, so keep surfing!*

Out on the Ledge

"HEY THERE, I'M GONNA CUTCHA EAR OFF," GRANDPA WOULD SAY, AS he gently grabbed my ear, pocketknife in hand, and with a big smile on his face.

That was always the greeting I got when I went over to visit my dear ol' grandpa. I knew he wouldn't do it; I could see the love behind that smile. So whenever we went over there, I looked for our playful greeting. Grandpa knew how to have fun, as he brought out his popcorn maker and offered us a Coca-Cola.

He grew up on a farm in Black Lake, Canada, and was one of 16 children. After coming to the United States, he was placed in an orphanage, his parents too poor to feed and care for all of their children. He ran away from the orphanage at the very young age of 16, and then met and married my grandma.

Grandpa eventually became a window washer in order to support the six children he and Grandma brought into the world, one of whom was my mother. During our visits Grandpa would tell us stories about his job washing windows. Washing windows may not sound like a very impressive job, but my grandpa washed the windows of two of Detroit's historical skyscrapers—the Book Building, which was 37 stories high, and the Buhl Building, which was 26 stories high.

We listened carefully to every word, as he told us of hanging out of every window, using nothing more than a leather belt to hold him. We were so fascinated that he decided to take us to the Book Building for a demonstration. We were 28 stories up when Grandpa opened a window, crawled out onto the ledge, and hooked the belt to two small hooks, one on each side of the window. My heart leapt as I looked out at him hanging there, nothing below to catch him if he should fall.

Taking his bucket of water and squeegee with him, he took the squeegee and soaked the window with water. With very quick and sure strokes he scraped off all the dirt, leaving the window shiny and clean. Grandpa looked like he loved what he was doing, and I was so proud of him that day. He tried to get my dad to go out onto the ledge, with warm thoughts of his son-in-law following in his footsteps. But, even though Grandpa was only 5'7" tall, those were footsteps Dad wasn't about to try and fill.

Grandpa washed every window in those two buildings for 50 years! He never used a scaffold like they do on some buildings today. He did get someone to follow in his footsteps after all. His son Tom also washed windows in those buildings, and today Tom's son continues the tradition out at Metro Airport in Detroit.

As I was working at my desk down at Hutzel Hospital one morning, two window washers asked if I would mind moving so that they could clean the windows.

I most respectfully moved, smiling, and proudly exclaimed, "My grandfather was a window washer!"

They asked, "Oh yeah, what was his name?"

When I told them, they both exclaimed, "We knew Romeo Beaudoin, and we know his son, and grandson, too. Nice people!" I was so proud that my grandpa and his family had earned such a positive reputation for themselves.

As I was driving home one day, I decided to drive through Detroit and look for the Book Building. To my delight I was able to find it. I started feeling very sentimental and just had to stop and take a look. I parked my car, put my money in the parking meter, and strolled into what they're now calling "The Book Tower." As I walked under the arch, the entrance to the building, I saw that the words "The Book Building" are still formed in the cement, so graciously.

As I walked in the doors, I marveled at the artwork on the ceilings, now being renovated; the gray marble on the walls; and the hand-crafted doors on the old elevators. I strolled into the elevator and up to the twenty-eighth floor, looking around like a kid in a candy store. Reminiscently, I walked over to the window and looked out over Detroit, just like we did with Grandpa so many years ago.

I could almost hear his voice, with our own familiar greeting. I could see him hanging there, from his leather belt, so proud. Oh how I miss my grandpa; it doesn't seem like he's been gone 10 years.

My grandpa taught me all about courage back then, and he showed an even greater courage as he walked another ledge in his battle with cancer so long ago. Most of all, he showed me love. The kind of love that a granddaughter will carry deep within her heart on her own journey through life, as she is faced with walking out on ledges of her own.

—LINDA FERRIS

 Linda is a registered nurse living in southeast Michigan. She, her now 90-year-old grandmother, and their entire family miss Grandpa and hold each and every memory of him forever close to their hearts.

Their Song

My parents worked hard to provide for their family of four daughters. They taught us the true value of marriage—that you worked through your problems and stuck together through it all.

They were married in 1944 during a time when things were hard. Before paying the preacher for his marriage ceremony, my daddy had $7 in his pocket. After paying the preacher, he had $3 and a comb to start their new life on.

In November of 1997, two days before Thanksgiving, my mother was diagnosed with lung cancer and an aortic aneurysm. With false smiles of happiness pasted on our faces, we assembled for our normal traditional holiday gathering. In the back of our minds, we all wondered, "Will this be our last?"

My mother was scheduled for surgery on December 20, 1997. The weekend before, she asked all of us children to please come by. She wanted to give us our Christmas gifts. She had made each of

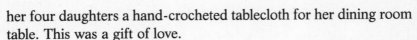

her four daughters a hand-crocheted tablecloth for her dining room table. This was a gift of love.

Do you realize how many stitches there are in a tablecloth? My father said she had worked night and day for the last year to get these gifts to us completed—the last gifts that she would ever crochet. She wanted us to have these heartfelt, everlasting gifts before she went in for surgery.

I held back my tears until I could leave her house.

My worst fears came true. On March 25, 1998, my mother left this earth for a better home. There are some days I miss her so much, I talk to her or touch the tablecloth she so lovingly made for me. I then get the strength to go on.

As hard as it was for me to learn to live without my mother, the loss for my father was unfathomable. Suddenly, after 54 years of being married to the same lady, he was facing life alone. He was a country man who had a wife and four daughters to cook and clean for him for all of these years. I never remember my father gracing the kitchen unless he was walking through to see what we might be having for dinner.

Suddenly my father became a cook (a quite good one, too) and a house cleaner. Isn't it amazing to realize what we can do when we need to? He handled my mother's death much better than any of us ever expected. My father visited the cemetery daily to clean around my mother's grave.

One day on his visit, he noticed a lady at the grave beside my mother's. She was visiting her late husband. As their eyes made contact across the granite headstones, he could see she was in pain and lonely—just like him. She shyly lowered her eyes.

My father's heart skipped a beat as he caught a glimpse of her sad, gentle smile. Suddenly feelings he thought had died made him want to protect her and make her smile again.

The sun suddenly appeared in all its rays of glory. It was as if someone were giving him the courage he needed to erase the distance between them. They engaged in polite conversation—then she was gone.

For days, my father thought of her sad, gentle smile and her sweet, southern grace. As it turns out, their paths had crossed many years before in our small hometown.

With trembling fingers my father took a chance. He dialed her number and prayed she'd answer. She did. She was happy to hear from him. Their phone conversations soon became their secret. They also kept their friendship a secret. For one year, their friendship blossomed, and none of us knew a thing about it.

Slowly their loneliness began to disappear. Suddenly their steps became sprier as their hearts beat faster. They realized that their lives had a new purpose. Instead of waiting to die, they had a reason to keep on living.

One morning my father awoke to the birds singing and a beautiful sunrise. He realized that whatever life he had left, he didn't want to live it alone. He wanted "Ms. Leo" by his side.

When I first learned of their relationship, and intention to marry, I felt pain. All of my life it had been my mama and daddy together. Suddenly I was seeing my father with someone else. The pain I felt was not anger against her—it was another realization that death is final, and my mother was not returning to this earth.

But then I came around and celebrated with him. How could I not love someone who makes my dad feel like living again? How could I not love someone who appears to be heaven sent? With their friends and family gathered around them, Ms. Leo honored my father by becoming his wife on February 12, 2000. Now their days are no longer lonely. They share companionship, laughter, and life. Their song is "One Day at a Time" because, they say, at their ages of 75 and 74, that's all you can do.

—GLENDA Q. SHEPARD

 Glenda lives with her husband of 23 years and their two teenage daughters on a small farm in Whigham, Georgia. She enjoys cooking and sharing recipes. She dreams of one day being able to slow down and travel to see the sights she has to date only read about.

Golf Course Romance

MY HUSBAND, ROY, HAD ALWAYS WANTED TO PLAY GOLF. I HAD HEARD the horrid "golf widow" stories and never encouraged the game. After quite a few years of marriage and raising three children, we were informed by our twin sons, Brad and Chad (now young adults), that they were taking up the sport of golf. Needless to say, they wanted their daddy to play with them. They begged and pleaded, but he had lost interest several years earlier.

Our sons surprised Roy with a set of golf clubs one Father's Day. During our vacation that year, the three of them played a round of golf. Since he had so much fun, he wanted to share the experience with me.

"Let's go to the golf course," he begged one Saturday afternoon.

"Why on earth would I want to play golf?" I asked.

"You can drive the cart," he replied. "Please." I saw a pitiful look on his face—just like a little boy with no money in a candy store.

My first thought was, "Sure I can, but I could also drive my car to the mall. It would be cooler and a lot more fun." I looked back at his sad face and finally agreed to go.

"Now how long will this take?" I asked with a twinge of resentment in my voice.

"We will only play nine holes," he said. He whistled as he got his equipment together. We headed for the green grass of the golf course.

I moaned as I got out of the car and sat down in the driver's seat of a little white golf cart. This was not my idea of a good time. Before I started up the engine, Roy started trying to teach me the rules of the road.

"What rules?" I shouted as I took off, driving full speed.

"Slow down," he begged. I laughed and kept driving. "You can only drive in designated spots," he sternly informed me.

"And who is going to stop me?" I joked. I was already feeling rebellious.

When we reached the tee box at hole number 1, he was shaking his head.

It was clear that he was relieved to get off of the speeding golf cart. He set up for his first swing while I watched, wondering why people think golf is so much fun. It looked mighty boring to me.

He hit the ball but had no idea where it went. For the next 15 minutes we searched for it.

"Oh, this is fun," I chided him.

"We'll just get another ball," he placated me, as he opened the pouch on his golf bag and pulled one out.

Back we went to the tee box. "This could take all afternoon," I grumbled to myself. When Roy hit the ball a second time, we found it down the fairway a little way. After quite a few strokes, the ball went into the hole. I can't remember the last time I saw my husband that happy.

"What was the big deal?" I wondered.

The driving game was on. We were off and speeding to the next hole. I was driving the cart, and he was walking. He said he needed the exercise, but I knew he was afraid of my driving. He spent a great deal of time hitting the ball and then looking for it, while I watched the squirrels and rabbits play.

Something entirely unexpected happened by the time we reached the fifth hole. We were laughing, harder than we had in many years. The financial stress associated with putting three kids through college was gone. The strain of "too much work and too little play" was replaced by happy hearts and smiling faces. To my utter amazement, a golf course romance was born.

By the time we got to hole number 6, I had fallen in love again. I felt like a young bride accompanying her prince charming. Suddenly, he looked so cute trying to keep up with that little white ball.

When we got to hole number 7, I sensed that he was watching me more than the ball. "Keep your eye on the ball," I reprimanded him.

"But I can't," he replied. "I like looking at you."

At that point, he decided that he would ride with me again. This time, he didn't get upset when I drove too fast. By the time we reached hole number 8, we were holding hands. I don't know if he was holding on for dear life or if he enjoyed holding my hand, but nevertheless, I liked it.

It had been a long while since we last held hands.

The last hole, number 9, was the best hole of all. Before he stepped off the cart, he leaned over and kissed me. "I'm glad you came," he said.

"I had so much fun. Can we come back next week?" I asked. A smile covered his face—and mine.

"Yes, and next time we'll play eighteen holes," he asserted. He smacked the ball and it soared off into the woods. We both giggled as we drove off to find yet another lost ball.

This time, it didn't matter to me. My husband was happy. I was enjoying his company. Golf was just a good excuse to be together. We were not only finding lost balls. We were finding each other again, too.

—NANCY GIBBS

Over the last couple of years, Roy's golf game has improved. Nancy now has her own set of clubs, so she has to admit—she's now the one chasing the balls.

She still prefers driving the cart, watching the wildlife, and spending time with her husband and very best friend.

Falling in Love Again

AFTER 16 YEARS OF MARRIAGE, I SUDDENLY FELL HEAD OVER HEELS IN love.

How wonderful to feel the joy of knowing that this is the one with whom you are destined to share the rest of your life. My heart beat quicker when I saw him. I cherished the times we were together, when we laughed, prayed, and planned.

My first husband, Richard, did not die. We did not divorce. I did not have an affair.

I suddenly fell head over heels in love with the man I married 16 years ago. Heart-pounding, romantic love—the kind of feeling that usually dies in a marriage that has weathered lost jobs, enormous financial difficulties, in-law problems, and 10 years of sorrow-filled infertility.

We've always had what we considered to be an outstanding marriage. After all, we were still together after 16 years, even though seven out of nine couples in our immediate family of parents and siblings had separated and/or divorced.

We began our marriage with a commitment to a lasting relationship. We participated willingly in premarital counseling to get us started on a solid foundation. As many of our friends' marriages began to shatter into thin shards of lost dreams, we stayed a couple.

So, as our sixteenth anniversary approached, we were together and happy. We didn't have devastating fights. We didn't have bitter secrets. Yet, something was missing.

I spent several days in depression, irritated that my husband didn't know what I needed without me having to tell him, yet not willing to tell him myself. Finally, once I saw that he noticed my coldness, I knew I had to share with him what was troubling me. After all, we were not a couple that kept secrets from one another.

I wrote him a long letter, relating my hurts, sorrows, and frustration that he spent more time and effort on his ministry and his teaching than he did with me. I poured my heart out to him, sharing with him feelings on paper that I had never said to him before.

I sat in my office for an hour, searching for courage to give Richard my letter. I held it tightly in my hand and walked into the living room, where he sat reading a book.

"Please read this," I asked. "Please read it now."

He looked at the letter I placed beside him and then at me.

"Okay," he said.

I left the room and went into the kitchen to wait.

Our precious daughter, six now, ran into the kitchen to show me her latest drawing. I stroked her hair, grateful for the miracle we'd been given through Michelle. We had adopted her at the age of nine months, and I wanted her to always know Richard and I loved one another.

I heard the rustle of paper as Richard read the letter. "How about a nap, sweetie," I suggested to Michelle.

It seemed like hours, but only 20 minutes after Richard read my letter, as our daughter napped, we talked.

I expected to hear a deep-felt apology. Instead, he explained to me that some of my past attitudes and angry responses toward him had caused him to pull away from me. He wanted to be closer to me, too. But he had closed his heart in self-defense.

More hurt than ever, I went to the bathroom to cry. I was devastated. I thought we had a good marriage, a happy one. Now what? How would we work this out?

Soon afterward, we sat together again, holding one another as he told me how he'd been praying while I'd been crying.

He had allowed words I'd said and actions he had disapproved of to build. He had been hurt and, rather than hurt me, kept his feelings to himself.

"I've never stopped loving you," he said. "And I never will. But your anger toward others, your bitterness at the way my family has hurt us, and the constant worry over finances have made me feel as if I'm married to a different person."

It hurt. I knew he was right, but it still hurt. "Then tell me what to do differently, so that you won't distance yourself from me," I pleaded. "Don't pull away from me. That just makes me more angry, bitter, and full of worry. Neither of us is perfect. We promised we wouldn't let our marriage be average like so many in our family. We promised we'd work things out together," I begged him.

"Then let's keep our promises," Richard said.

Once he admitted his feelings, and his conditional love, the walls came down. That evening, when Michelle had gone to bed, we spent hours talking.

It helped us enormously that this was not just *my* desire to fall in love again with my husband. My husband shared my longing to be reconnected in a deeper way. A few weeks earlier when he had attended a men's conference, he had prayed, "I want to fall in love with my wife again."

From that day forward, our longtime marriage was given a high-voltage charge. Our relationship grew even stronger than ever before. That day was only the beginning.

Two weeks later, we joined a marriage class at church. The study was designed for marriage communication. Each week we came home and talked about our dreams, our fears, our hopes. We wrote letters to one another, telling of the things we admired most about each other. The class drew us even closer together.

On our sixteenth anniversary, at a romantic candlelit restaurant, my husband placed a small box in my hand.

"I'd marry you all over again," he said.

"Me too!" I replied.

"Will you?" he asked, taking my hand. "Will you marry me again?"

My beloved husband had already begun making plans for a second wedding ceremony. He filled me in on his dream, and his plans, and I was elated.

With Michelle, now seven years old, as a witness, 12 weeks later on Easter weekend (16 years, 3 months, and 22 days after the first time we committed to be together for the rest of our lives), we stood before our friends and family and renewed our wedding vows.

Many people yearn to marry the love of their life—their best friend and soulmate. I am one of the lucky ones. I was able to do it twice.

They say that romantic love fades because once you actually know the man or woman you married, it's not easy to maintain the illusions of perfection we hold in the beginning.

This time, I fell in love with my eyes completely open. I know this man I am in love with, and I love him even more.

—KATHRYN LAY

One of Kathyrn's favorite love songs is an oldy—"When I Fall in Love." It played while she walked down the aisle at her wedding . . . the second one.

Richard teaches English as a Second Language in a high school. He and Kathy run a ministry together at their church to help refugees and immigrants. He enjoys storm chasing, and Kathy is a full-time freelance writer. Michelle, now nine, is homeschooled and loves animals and art. They live in Texas. Kathryn and Richard are still falling in love, every day.

$\mathcal{L}$ove That Heals

WHEN SHE RANG ME TO MAKE AN APPOINTMENT FOR COUNSELING, SHE was bright and full of quirky self-humor, but I could detect her brittleness. Even over the phone, I could tell she was hurting. She presented for the consultation wearing the big smile she always showed to the world, but her huge, luminous brown eyes reflected great pain.

It had not been that long since her second marriage had ended in divorce. Drugs and alcohol had played a significant part in her life, as the buried issues of the past frequently reared up and overwhelmed her. She had relinquished the only child of her first marriage to her ex-husband and his new wife so the girl could grow up in a regular family, with her stepbrothers and stepsisters. She visited, often, but leaving was harder each time.

"Just help me work through a few things," she said. "I'll be fine. I'm a survivor and I'm kicking the habit," she reassured me— or was she reassuring herself?

She was gutsy and determined. Occasionally, I would receive an after-hours call of pain-wracked sobbing, but she got employment, she kept the job, and she made new friends. She read, she meditated, and she took courses to improve her life.

Then, one day, she and her flatmate took in a third person to share the rent, a younger man who had finally broken free from an unhappy marriage.

In spite of the age difference, there was an instant attraction between them. The other flatmate unexpectedly moved away, and my client and the young man progressed from being tenants-in-common, to inseparable friends, and then, to lovers.

He was gentle, kind, and caring. He helped to rebuild those areas within her that early life and the last marriage had smashed down. He was patient when, at times, she would scream, hurl accusations at him, and reject the mental intimacy she so desperately craved. She was consumed by fear: fear that it would, again, end in failure; fear that he would change from the wonderful person he was to a monster she was more familiar with; fear that she would disappoint him and let him down; fear that he would seek the company of a younger woman.

Over the next few years, she ran away—frequently—but he was always there, waiting for her, ready to forgive. Slowly, she began to realize that she was wanted and needed. The relationship became reciprocal; she had a role she could fulfill. When he had problems with his ex-wife, who sometimes denied him child access, or with his work, she offered him strength, encouragement, and support.

She began to discover that he had started to rely on her. Within this loving relationship, she grew calmer and began to radiate a glow that I hadn't seen in her face before.

He asked her to marry him—several times—but she always refused, citing the 10 years between them and her failure rate. But he was stubborn and persistent, and, finally, eight years after they had met, she asked me in my capacity as head of my church to officiate at their wedding in March.

It was a thrilling occasion to see this happy, laughing, trouble-free lady alight with love; to know that after all she had been through, all she had overcome, she had been given the blessing, the ultimate reward of finding her soulmate. The small gathering of family and friends was equally elated. This wedding was so much more than just the culmination of a romance: It was a triumph of the spirit.

They went away for a couple of days of honeymooning, and then it was back to work. They rented a house that was nearer to the sea, yet still allowed her to grow vegetables in her garden. She switched from casual to permanent job status; he got a promotion. They were wonderfully happy and life was good.

Later that year, I went away on a Christmas vacation. The cell phone was malfunctioning and the remote access for my home answering machine simply refused to operate, so I was totally out of touch with my clients while I was gone. When I returned, the first thing I did was check the messages that had accumulated in my absence.

Sandwiched among the routine calls was one from my client-turned-friend. Her voice was neutral, but knowing her as well as I did, I was acutely aware of the control she had used in the simple words:

"Would you phone me, please . . ."

I rang, immediately. "What's wrong?"

She was wooden, seemingly unemotional although screaming inside.

"The doctor says he has maybe three months to live," she replied. "It's melanoma."

I still shiver when I recollect that call.

She took a leave from work and devoted herself, full-time, to caring for her husband. She fed him vitamins, herbs, and health foods. They pored over self-help and self-cure books together. I meditated with them both. She was a tower of strength, an inspiration. She knew what he wanted, without his having to ask. She understood him completely, and he let her take control as his vitality drained, inexorably, from him.

The pace of the disease was terrifying, from the initial swelling spotted in September—and declared by the doctor to be harmless—to the multitude of lumps that sprouted internally and externally at Christmas, the lymphatic breakdown, and, finally, the insidious wasting away that is typical of all cancers.

His hold on life was diminishing before our eyes. A hunky sports enthusiast, he deteriorated to a raw-nerved skeleton—but he smiled. He even laughed—after the morphine kicked in.

The weaker he got, physically, the stronger he became, mentally—because of her and the calmness and strength she exuded. She didn't go to pieces; she got on with making things as easy as possible for him. She helped him to face what was coming. She had stared death in the face, many times, and she knew there was always a new beginning.

She wanted him to be fully prepared and to not have to worry about leaving those he loved. She brought me in to talk to him and his grieving and bewildered sisters, so I could help them deal with their fears and concerns with him as a witness. She even formed a connection with his ex-wife, and with her, spent hours preparing his daughter for his death.

He was totally at peace when he passed over—with her beside him, holding his hands.

I was asked to facilitate the funeral only 13 months after facilitating their wedding. The chapel was crowded. Family, friends, workmates of them both crammed into the pews and filled the doorway. She sat in the front, smiling and composed, but with those huge brown eyes riveted on me, as if she could connect back to him through me, through my words.

She brought his dog with her, the friend that had been so much a part of his last days. When they carried the coffin out of the building, she walked with her back straight and her head held high. It wasn't raining, but a huge rainbow filled the sky, the same image that had come to me when I meditated about him the night before.

One month later, we went back to the cemetery for a ceremonial scattering of the ashes. As she tenderly scooped out handfuls of the gray and white dust, she thanked him for staying with her as long as he did; for believing in her and for all that he had taught her. She told him that she would not fail him; that she would make a new life for herself, founded on his love and wisdom. She assured him that he would be part of her forever.

With the superannuation payout from her late husband's estate and the financial help of her son-in-law, she bought herself a house that would have appealed to her late husband, "so that he can come and visit any time he wishes," with room for the dog and cats he loved to run free.

The radiant glow has been replaced by a serene inner strength, and, through her efforts, his daughter and sisters have come to terms with their loss. Longtime family hurts and resentments have been cleared up, and she has forged new bonds between them all.

The time my client and friend spent with her husband was short, but their union contained more joy and depth than most people are ever lucky enough to know. After a lifetime of despair, she was blessed by the healing of perfect and total love.

—JAIME STRAUSS

Jaime Strauss lives in Australia and is a professional counselor and sex therapist and has guested many times on TV and talk-back radio shows. Being blessed with the power to heal and a heightened spiritual awareness, she founded The Peoples' Church of Truth, and with her love of writing, creates individual services for all occasions.

Emotional Reunion

I WAS EIGHT MONTHS PREGNANT WHEN MY HUSBAND TOLD ME THAT the aircraft carrier USS *Independence* was heading out on a four-month deployment in one month. Tears streamed down my face. "But you won't be here when the baby is born?" I cried. He wiped my tears, held me tightly, and told me that he would talk to his commander.

The good news was that he could stay for two weeks after the baby was born. The bad news was that we were living in Japan. I had no family or close friends to support me, and my husband was leaving for four months shortly after the birth of his first child. I spent many nights crying and worrying about what I would do. Should I stay in Japan by myself and be a single mom for four months, or should I return home, flying the 16 hours to Boston with a newborn and a dog?

We had our baby, a beautiful, healthy boy whom we named Eric. We treasured every moment as a family because we both knew that soon, very soon, our family would be torn apart, one way or another. Jeff made plans to meet the carrier in Singapore. I decided to make the dreadful trip home to be with family.

I was scared, tired, and angry. My husband would miss the first four months of his son's life. Over and over I reminded myself that we all had to make sacrifices because of Jeff's career. We married knowing that Jeff would be gone a lot, and as real as it was, I tried to deny this fact.

Jeff drove me, Eric, and our dog, Max, to Narita Airport, one of the busiest airports in the world. The place swarmed with people all in a hurry to leave. I clung to Jeff every inch of the way. We got Max taken care of in customs and got us through the terminal. We had some moments to spare before it was time to board.

I couldn't look at Jeff without crying. I couldn't talk without choking up.

Really, we didn't have to say anything. We both knew how each of us felt. He hugged me tight. I could tell he didn't want to send me away. He didn't want to leave his family. Tears welled in his eyes, but wanting to be strong for me, he held them back.

When they called my flight I lifted Eric in his carrier and faced Jeff. The tears dropped like a leaky faucet. I couldn't get the words out. Exhausted from being a new mom and all that comes with it, I wrapped my arms around Jeff. I didn't want to let him go, but even if I stayed, he'd be leaving in a couple of days. He kissed me and said, "I love you and I'll be in touch as often as I can." Then he bent down and kissed his sleeping son. I didn't look at Jeff again. I picked up Eric and walked toward the plane, never looking back. I knew that if I did, I'd run to Jeff and not leave Japan.

I told myself, "Don't cry in public, everyone is looking at you," but I didn't care. "Let them look," I thought. I deserve to cry!

My family was anxiously awaiting our arrival in Boston. I couldn't let them down. I boarded the plane, tears rolling steadily, dripping on Eric, my sweater, and my tickets. I couldn't talk to the stewards, the words just got choked in the middle of my throat. I'm sure they'd seen this many times before. I found my seat and collapsed. Eric, buckled safely in the seat next to mine, gurgled a little, not knowing the full extent of what had just happened. Thankfully, he slept for hours and so did I.

The weeks that followed were filled with joy and sadness. I wasn't getting much sleep because of the hours Eric was keeping, but my family, eager and helpful, were doing what they could to help me. I missed Jeff terribly. He called when he could from the different ports, but port calls were few and far between. I wrote him a letter every day and anxiously waited by the mailbox for his letters to arrive. Weeks went by without a word, and I started thinking the worst—had Jeff already forgotten us? How could he go this long without writing?

Finally, just as I was losing all hope, I received my first letter a month after we separated. I later learned that this was not unusual for the military's mail system—it was very slow. The letter was three pages long and not filled with what Jeff was doing or where he had been, but filled with love and hope and how much he missed his family. This time, the tears that dripped down my cheeks and wet my baby and my sweater were ones of happiness.

Those letters, which came regularly from that point forward, kept me going day to day, week to week.

I tried not to watch the news. It was during Operation Southern Watch, and I knew Jeff would be flying over Iraq. There was always a chance that I might not ever see him again. Watching the news only confirmed my worries. What would I do if something were to happen? How awful to think that Eric would never know his father. If I chose to dwell on these things, it would have driven me mad. Instead I focused on our reunion and making Jeff as much a part of his son's life as possible.

I videotaped Eric and every new thing he achieved—his first laugh, holding his head up, grabbing toys. Of course, it took me several tries because I'd always end up crying at the end of the video. I didn't want Jeff to worry about me. I wanted him to see a happy wife.

I audiotaped Eric's little noises and "talked" some of my letters to him, so he could hear my voice. I wrote love letters filled with words of encouragement and the excitement I felt of seeing him again.

His letters expressed the same enthusiasm. He missed us terribly and couldn't wait to be a family again.

After three and a half months passed, Eric, our dog, and I made the long, tiring trek back to Japan. Jeff was due home in two weeks. That left me just enough time to get settled back in and "fixed up" for our reunion. I checked each day off the calendar and danced with Eric in the living room, singing "Daddy's coming home!" Eric squealed and laughed a lot. I think maybe he knew.

The day Jeff arrived was glorious. It was the end of March; cool yet sunny and the sky as clear as it can get. The other wives and I hurried to the hangar with children in tow and anxiously awaited the arrival. We heard rumbles as jets flew over the base. Finally, over the radio, we heard "On deck, five minutes." Laughter and claps filled the ready room, where we were waiting. I stuffed yellow earplugs into Eric's tiny ears. We rushed through the hangar and out to the flight line. Heads peered for the sky. Looking, listening, and waiting.

"There!" shouted one wife as she pointed to the sky. I looked up and saw an awesome sight. Four F-14s flying in formation, coming in very fast for the break. One by one they split off. I knew Jeff was in one of the jets. My heart raced faster and faster.

"Land the darn plane!" I mumbled and clenched my teeth. Each jet rolled down the runway, and they parked side by side.

The pilots climbed out and made their way to us. I spotted Jeff immediately and grabbed Eric out of his stroller. Jeff took off his helmet and ran toward us. Sweat mixed with tears as he hugged Eric and me. When we looked up, cameras surrounded us. Japanese television and the base newspaper shoved microphones into our faces. We didn't care. We kissed like we had never kissed before. Then Jeff took Eric in his arms, looked hard into his eyes, and said, "He looks just like me."

Jeff didn't let me out of his sight or let Eric out of his arms for the rest of the day. We were all home, a family again, and that's all that mattered. Eventually, we'd have to prepare for the next separation, but this wasn't the time to think about that.

The next day on the front page of the newspaper was a picture of Jeff, Eric, and me, huddled together, smiling. The caption said, "Emotional Reunions." I still treasure that picture today. It reminds me of how we survived one of the toughest separations in our family's life. We stuck together in spirit even though we were physically apart, and we made it.

That love has held us together in some of the roughest times of our marriage. That trust has never been broken because we know just how much it would hurt the other person. We promised each other that our marriage would always come first, then our family, because without a solid foundation, our family would suffer.

Today, Jeff is working in private industry, and he travels from time to time. Now, when Jeff is away from home on business, it's okay. I know that nothing could be as bad as what we had endured during those long four months when he was in the military.

In a way, now I look forward to Jeff's leaving. It never allows us to take each other for granted. I buy his favorite candy and stick love letters in his suitcase. He leaves something special for me under my pillow. And, there is nothing like the reunion after time apart.

Our separations have allowed our love to grow deeper and richer and have helped us to remember to treasure every moment we have together.

—JENNIFER B. REED

Jennifer and Jeff Reed currently reside in Maryland with their two children, Eric, who is now 7, and Emma, who is 5. Jeff left the military after serving for eight years as a Naval Flight Officer. He decided that being with his family was more important than flying jets. He now works as a program manager for a major aerospace corporation. Jennifer writes for children's magazines and recently had her first children's novel and a children's anthology accepted for publication. Together, Jennifer and Jeff have developed a children's online magazine called Wee Ones.

$\mathcal{R}$estart Button

"CAN WE PRESS THE RESTART BUTTON TODAY?" MY 27-YEAR-OLD daughter, Jen, asked, climbing back into her Jeep and starting toward the freeway out of the city. Haste had unraveled her calm as we sped to join other pottery students from her class for an early morning outing to a mountain town. She hadn't seemed cranky to me, but I stroked her shoulder and agreed, "We can restart the day anytime."

As we drove through the quaint countryside, I marveled how Jen had changed. We had come out of the chilly fog of the teenage years' clashes into the warm sunlight of mutual understanding in her adulthood. My once belligerent teen had bloomed into a delightful companion.

That day we toured the artist's studio, videoed his lecture, and laughed over lunch. She dropped me off at my High Desert home on her way back to the city. I felt as if I had spent the day with a very dear friend. It was wonderful, and I dropped her an e-mail thanking her for having Mom along.

We had made a habit of me visiting her in Long Beach every six weeks, but when I called her to plan our next get-together, she cut me off mid-sentence.

"I don't think I want to see you for a while," she curtly informed me. Her brisk final tone signaled "back off" as clearly as warning lights.

Hurt and shocked at her out-of-the-blue rejection, I got off the phone and had a good boo-hoo in the shower. I reviewed my behavior with her. I could not pinpoint what annoyed her, and she didn't give me a clue on the phone. Clearly Jen did not want to talk to me for a while.

Gently, the Lord reminded me how many of His children reject him every day. I would have to be patient and allow my daughter the space that she needed.

Months went by with short bursts of phone contact, but little more. Jen immersed herself in her career, acquired a new house-mate, and moved to new quarters. Although I missed her terribly, I devoted myself to the field of dreams in front of me and tilled my own acre, writing and mentoring other writers. I left my problem with Jen in the lap of the Lord. He mends hearts better than I can.

One day, six months after Jen had cut me off, she called and breezily invited my husband and I to visit her new place.

Praying to keep my expectations low, to guard against disappointment, my husband, Clarence, and I drove to Long Beach. Jen greeted us warmly and ushered us through her new digs. We trooped after her, admiring her artistic flair.

In her kitchen window box, I noticed a stunning slate blue glass-fronted memory box. It startled me to see a black-and-white picture of my mother and me as a little girl propped up inside the box, with a silver French wire ribbon twining between it and a blue-and-gold suspended heart.

Since my mother chooses to be a distant figure in my life, I didn't know what to make of the art. It was a chillingly ironic reminder of my strained relationship with Jen.

My daughter stood next to me and tipped her chin toward the box. "I made it for you."

I stared at it, wondering what to make of this gift after the grief of her rejection. "It's beautiful, Jen, you are so talented." I gulped.

Gently lifting the box down and placing it in my hands, she urged. "Look more closely."

The interior was lined in posh paper printed in a font of rounded Irish calligraphy, words rich with remembrance to me:

Butterflies, apple pie,
Ireland, the coziness of naps, cats, trellis tea parties.

"I designed the paper on my computer," she whispered.

It astonished me that she recalled so many little details in my life. I set the box down and drew Jen into my arms, embracing her while tears washed away the sting of rejection. We hugged a long time.

The only explanation that Jen could offer for her requested season of distance was that during our much-enjoyed outing, old teenage feelings washed over her and she needed to reassert her independence from me.

Jen and I made the choice to push the restart button on that day, and we have grown closer ever since. When she needed space from me, she wasn't turning the button off. She was simply pausing it, deepening her love for me and herself, and restarting the button when she was ready for another level of intimacy with me than we enjoyed before.

There was, for a while, a time when we needed, as Kahlil Gibran says, "space in our togetherness." And that's okay. Because whenever I look now at my treasure box sitting in my bookshelf above my desk where I write, it tells me, "I love you Mother, I value your history, and I value you."

Thank goodness for restart buttons.

—ELLEN BERGH

Ellen Bergh is a speaker and author who writes "Mom in the Mirror," a column encouraging other child abuse survivors. Her work appears in the God's Abundance series, and she is a staff writer for Mojave Desert News.

$\mathscr{N}$ot Now, My Love

THE GREATEST LOVE STORY OF MY LIFE STARTED IN A CHAT ROOM ON the Internet.

I received a private message from a guy named Chris who lived in California. I live in Florida. We got to chatting online, and he told me that he was going to be visiting Florida in a couple of weeks for a business trip. He informed me that usually when he knew that his company was sending him to another state for a convention, he tried to meet someone from a chat room in that area, to have someone to show him around. He often stayed a few extra days to see a part of the country he hadn't seen before.

After chatting online with him several more times, I decided to call him. I remember thinking, "What am I doing talking to this guy? I don't even know him."

Over the next couple of weeks or so, we talked often. Then came the time for Chris to arrive in Florida. The first few days he was here he was attending his conference for work, and I didn't see him. On Wednesday of that week, he called me. He had gotten a hotel room not too far from my house, and we talked about our plans for the following day to visit Busch Gardens, a local theme park. He told me that he would call me later that evening and we hung up.

The phone rang almost immediately, and it was Chris again. He said, "I think we would have fun going to Busch Gardens, but I think we would have a better time if you let your girls [I have two daughters] skip school and we take them to Disney World."

I didn't know what to say or to think. I was a single mother and had never been able to afford to take my children to Disney. When I began to object, he offered to pick up the cost. After a few minutes, I agreed to take him up on his generous offer. I hung up the phone, and then I started to panic. "What was I thinking? I don't know this guy and I am going to jump in a car with my kids and him and head to Disney?"

I called up my best friend, Dawn, and told her the story. She encouraged me to meet him that evening, before I agreed to spend the entire day with him at Disney World. I called him back, and he agreed to come to my home to briefly meet. Some people might wonder why I wasn't concerned about inviting a stranger to my home, but I guess it's because he no longer felt like a stranger. I had talked to him so many times on the phone, I trusted him.

He arrived at my home as planned. I knew after only a few moments that we would have a fabulous day at Disney World. I was immediately comfortable in his presence. We made plans for the next day, and I was so excited that evening, I could barely sleep. I kept wondering, "Why is this man being so generous to a woman and her kids whom he barely knows?"

We arrived at Disney World bright and early the next morning. My kids were elated. While riding on the ferryboat to the Magic Kingdom, my youngest daughter said to me, "Mom, this is a ferryboat, right?"

"Yes," I said.

"Then where are all the fairies?" she asked.

We had a wonderful day, and my kids absolutely loved Chris. And, so did I.

Toward the end of the day, while we were on the Haunted House ride, he touched my hand.

I cannot explain to you how I felt at that moment. We held hands on and off throughout the rest of the day. We had a full day at Disney, staying until the fireworks went off. My kids were beat! On the way home, they fell asleep in the car.

When we arrived at my house, Chris carried the little one upstairs for me and placed her in her bed. After both the girls were in bed, we went to the living room to talk. I told him how much I appreciated the wonderful day he had given my girls and me. It almost felt like a scene out of a Disney movie! He in turn told me how much fun he had had and how we already felt like a family to him.

We parted, planning to lunch the next day before he left for California. I couldn't wait to see him again.

Chris came over early, and, as planned, we went shopping and to lunch. He asked if he could go with me to pick up my girls from school so that he could see them again before he left. We did so, and then took them to McDonald's, where we sat, mostly in silence, knowing that he had to leave in a couple of hours. He drove us back to our house and gave the girls some gifts he had bought for them at the mall. And then it was time to say goodbye.

I didn't know if I would ever even see Chris again. My heart was breaking. I had only known him a few weeks and been in his company for 40 hours, and yet, somehow, so unexpectedly, he had deeply touched my heart, and the girls' hearts.

What was the purpose of our connection? I cannot relocate to California because of my children, who are 5 and 10 years old. Their fathers would never approve of them moving out of the state. Chris has a life in California that he has been working for—a very good job, lifetime friends, and sports activities like skiing that he can't do in Florida.

We talked every day after he got home, some days, several times a day.

Soon we were telling each other, "I love you," and talking about whether there was any way to be together. That was a year ago, and we have yet to find a way. I have dated others since Chris, but no one else has come close to touching me in the same way. Chris told me that he figures we'll be together someday, even if it's after we have lived most of our lives with someone else.

Love is a difficult thing. Loving Chris means not only that I long to be with him, but that I wouldn't ask him to make all the sacrifices he would need to in order to be with me and the girls. And since my first loyalty is to my children, I can't just pick up and leave Florida to follow my heart. That's the stuff of fairy tales.

Maybe with love, there isn't always a happy ending. Or maybe, since in a fairy tale, the boy and the girl always wind up together, our fairy tale just hasn't ended yet.

For now, I take comfort in knowing that no matter where I go or what I do, there is a very special man who lives in California who owns a piece of my heart.

—MARLISA HODGE

 Marlisa lives in Florida with her two daughters and works as a nurse.

Favorite Song

IT WAS CHRISTMAS EVE 1990 IN SAUDI ARABIA. THE MOOD THAT evening was very gloomy, for me and for all of the other soldiers stationed there. Every part of my body ached from loneliness. It was my first Christmas away from home.

It was my first Christmas away from my father, Robert Anderson, the man whom I treasured and admired for so many years.

This wasn't the first night I began to miss him; it was four months prior to this that I learned what aching for someone who is gone feels like. My battalion was on alert for deployment, and I was in Texas at the time. I returned to the barracks when I received the phone call that would change my life forever.

My father had had a heart attack, and he was in the hospital in Michigan, in critical condition. I flew from Texas to Michigan on the earliest flight out, hoping and praying that he would still be alive. I had five wonderful days with him, and I visited him as much as I could. Then it happened; he had another heart attack.

They flew him by helicopter to another hospital 45 minutes away, where they were better equipped to perform the surgery he needed. My mother, grandfather, and I drove as fast as we could to meet him at the hospital. I held his hand and looked into his eyes before he went into surgery. I felt a connection with him like I never felt before. I told him how much I loved him and that I would see him soon.

My heart ached as I watched them roll him away. That was the last time I ever saw him alive.

Now, four months later, it was Christmas time, and I was away from home. How could I be strong for my troops when all I wanted was to be in my father's arms again? I wanted to be in the comfort of my own home, smelling my father's cooking while listening to the laughter of my brothers.

I lay staring at my cassette tape for what seemed like hours. My friend, Julie, another soldier, finally asked me if I wanted to play the song on her stereo system. I hesitated at first but then I said yes.

Everyone in the tent stood in a circle and held hands. The tape began, and we listened to the music of "Silent Night" by the Temptations.

When the song began I was flooded with memories of my childhood. As a family, we always listened to this song on Christmas Eve. When I was younger my father would dance with me to the song. I felt as if he was singing to only me, and we were the only ones in the room. He made me feel so important and so very special. I was then, and always will be, daddy's little girl.

I began to cry out loud. I cried for the situation I was in, for my father, and for all the soldiers who were separated from their families. As I looked around, I noticed everyone else had tears streaming down their faces, too. We kept singing and crying until the last note of the tune.

When the music finished, there was a strange silence in the tent. After a few moments of silence, people began to talk and eventually began to laugh.

It was exactly what we needed. We realized that we were in similar situations, but one thing we had in common was each other. An incredible bond formed among us that night, carrying us through the next six months.

To this day on Christmas Eve I listen to "Silent Night" by the Temptations.

The first time I hear it I always cry for my father. This year when I heard the song it was even more special because I, too, asked my daughter to dance with me to the song. Maybe someday she will realize how much that dance meant to me. Each year I receive strength and a sense of peace from listening to the song "Silent Night." It is the strength that I am sure my father wanted me to have.

—STEFANIE JANUARY

Stefanie was in the army for nine and a half years. Her job title was SSGT, while being a linguist. She met her husband, Montral, while stationed in Saudi Arabia.

After coming back to the states, Stefanie and Montral married. They have two beautiful daughters, Pamela and Jessica. Stefanie is taking college courses and was asked to write a story about a favorite song, and why it is a favorite. From that, came this heartwarming story.

*B*lue Eyes

I MET MY HUSBAND, ADAM, AT THE WEDDING OF SOME MUTUAL FRIENDS at the Four Seasons in my hometown, Washington, D.C. Adam tells me that we were introduced at a picnic the day of the wedding, but I don't really remember this momentous event, which is still a bone of contention between us. I most certainly do remember him from the wedding, however.

The bride and groom cut through the social protocol and simply put the single people at the same table. When he walked up to the table in his black tuxedo, I almost fainted. The first thing I noticed was his eyes. They were the kind of ocean blue that you can see only in Bermuda or other exotic places. He had a confidence about him as he joked with his friends and an animation that grabbed my undivided attention.

I wanted to talk to Adam right away, but he was seated on the other side of the table. Luckily I ended up in a conversation with one of his friends, who asked me the fateful question, "What is your favorite movie?" A bit underwhelmed with the level of conversation, I aloofly said, "You haven't heard of it, *Spinal Tap.*" This man looked at me with such shock.

"You're kidding, you've seen *Spinal Tap*?" he exclaimed.

"Yes, many times," I assured him.

Suddenly he summoned my dream boy. "Adam, come over here, you won't believe this," he shouted.

The two of them, my future husband and his drunken friend, proceeded to act out the entire movie for me, word for word. I laughed harder during that hour than all four years of college combined—and I laughed a lot in college. By the end of this performance, I was completely in love. Adam seemed pretty smitten with me, too, except that he had been doing shots of tequila for the last several hours, so he could have been infatuated with just about anybody at that point. I gave him my phone number and told him to call me, which he did the next morning. I was elated.

Since Adam was from New York, I took him on a tour of Washington, D.C., which included a make-out session at the Lincoln Memorial. If I could go back to any moment in my life, it would be that one—kissing Adam for the first time in front of Honest Abe in the summer of 1990. Now *that* is happiness.

On July 7, 2000, we celebrated a full decade together. In that time we have dated, cohabitated, married, and created a beautiful two-year-old boy, Elias. We still celebrate the day that we met and consider that our real anniversary.

Adam taught me the value of staying when things got uncomfortable and difficult, and not moving on to the next guy. Adam has everything in a partner that I wanted: understanding, sweetness, inclusiveness, affection, and a very good sense of humor, which we have needed over the years.

Now, 10 years later, we are full-fledged grownups, for better or worse. We have so many responsibilities and pressures that we have, like many couples, become more like business partners than the lovers we used to be.

We pay our bills, work like dogs, change diapers, play with our son, do errands, and when we can find a free second—we sleep.

When our son comes in to wake us up in the morning, we are so tired that we can barely move. And when we have another child, God willing, we expect to give up sleeping altogether.

In the span of 10 years, we have gone from being passionate lovers to each other's life raft. As our needs have changed, so have we. We are still lovers when we can find the time and the energy, but the rest of the time we keep each other afloat. Eventually, we will be past this stage of small children and hectic schedules and will probably look back and actually miss it.

In the meantime, our marriage is relegated to the occasional date night and the short time we have after our son goes to bed and we resume working at our respective computers.

But, even so, I'll say this: Adam's incredible blue eyes still give me that feeling I had when we first met—that stupid schoolgirl crush. When we are old and decrepit, and, I pray, still together, those eyes will still be my home. They give me a place of constancy, warmth, and love.

—AMY BOWLES-REYER

Amy Bowles-Reyer is a freelance writer and Web consultant living in Bethesda, Maryland, with her husband Adam and their green-eyed son Elias.

*L*ove Far Beyond the Physical

I HAD BEEN DIVORCED FOR SEVERAL YEARS AND HAD PROCLAIMED THAT I would never marry again. Little did I know that I would marry again, to the sweetest man in the world.

Nearly five years ago I was singing in a combination choir from the three sister churches in our area. We were rehearsing at my then home church, the site of our special Thanksgiving service. No one seemed to question that I could learn the alto parts to the songs; nor did anyone seem bothered by my use of Braille words for the music.

Eventually it came time to rehearse lining up and moving from our seats to our standing position. Most choirs do this as a matter of course, and I have sung in many choirs around the city with no catastrophic consequences.

But my consistent experience has been that, whenever it comes to moving around, suddenly somebody panics—even though I have a long white cane and use it effectively.

As usual, on the day in question someone suddenly realized that I was at the head of the line of altos and that I would be standing at the end of the line near the steps that led off the platform. This fact did not bother me. I knew I could lead the section to the right spot, and I knew that I could stop before reaching the top of the steps by using my common sense and my cane.

When I assured the group that I could do this, suggestions came like: "Let's put someone else in front of Laurie for her to follow. That will be safer for all of us." "Laurie, you could stay in your seat and just rise with the rest of us to sing. You know your part, so you can sing from wherever you are. It won't matter." "Why don't you make it easier for all of us?"

I felt an avalanche of well-intended solutions almost smothering me. I felt totally embarrassed having this much attention unnecessarily focused on me.

The words "It won't matter" struck me like a bullet, right in the middle of my broken heart. I suddenly heard myself ask, quite strongly, "Well, what about my dignity?"

What followed was that deafening silence with which many of us are far too familiar. Had I now been totally rejected, or was there an inaudible, "Oh! I never thought about that"?

The silence seemed to last longer than any of the pieces we were to sing. I prayed fervently to the Holy Spirit, who in my understanding has never addressed blindness negatively. God has given me a good mind; I trusted that He would give me the necessary words to help us move on.

Then I broke the silence by laughingly saying that I didn't understand why people thought I couldn't walk when it was my eyes that didn't work properly. We got it worked out.

I didn't see the tall, thin, bearded man leaning against the piano so he wouldn't fall. Most people, on seeing him, would describe him as "fragile." In fact, that was the term I would hear many times emanating from the mouths of the medical community.

There was also someone in the soprano section, a very outgoing psychiatric nurse named Marilyn, who observed the aforementioned incident. She ran up to me after rehearsal and threw her arms around me, shouting, "Good for you for standing up for yourself!" She wanted to get to know me better, so she offered me a ride to the next rehearsal. By that time, unbeknownst to me, matchmaking was on her mind.

Before our third rehearsal, Marilyn called me, saying that she could not give me a ride, but she had talked to a Jim Merryfield, a very shy man, who had agreed to help me out. He had also witnessed the event, perceived my pain, related to it, and admired my standing up to it in spite of fear, and our mutual respect had begun.

When Jim and I first met, he carried with him what is now a four-page medical history that he quite proudly showed people he thought wouldn't "melt" upon reading it. He read it to me! I was so glad I had met him first before meeting his medical history—13 years of kidney dialysis, kidney transplant, constant back pain from scoliosis and botched surgeries, triple heart bypass with an automatic implantable cardiac defibrillator, lymphoma, multiple infections of an intensive-care degree—and he had died innumerable times (he remembers two occasions in which he struggled ferociously to stay alive).

We grew closer ever so quietly. Then one evening we walked in Mt. Vernon Gardens, a replica of the original in Omaha, Nebraska, where we lived at the time. Later, as we were sitting in the car near a lake, Jim noticed a look on my face and asked what I was thinking. I was afraid to say, but we both knew. He felt the same way!

We began to attend meaningful events as a couple, such as our state convention of the National Federation of the Blind, in October, and Thanksgiving at my sister's.

We became engaged during a church service on December 22, 1996. We chose Mt. Vernon Gardens as the site for our wedding and May 24, 1997, as the date.

My bliss was shattered the very next day, so near to Christmas, when my daughter, Lynden, rejected the notion of me marrying Jim. She didn't want me to marry anyone, especially Jim. She wanted me to find a supposedly able-bodied, well-to-to doctor/lawyer-type, and Jim seemed more like a hippie to her. She feared that my love for Jim would take away my love for her, though I attempted to reassure her that my well of love was unending.

She slumped into a dangerous depression for which outside counseling became necessary. She vowed she would not move with us or attend our wedding. What had I done?

Six days before the wedding, we ordered Jim's tux. We were both exhausted from preparations but figured we would rest soon. That night, unbeknownst to me, Jim called 911 as he had trouble breathing and was coughing up blood. I slept soundly that night and woke up later than usual. We usually checked in by phone around noon, so when I arose, I checked my phone messages. How startled I was by the message! Jim was in intensive care, and the nurses urged me to come to the hospital! In shock, I called our minister, who helped drive me to the hospital. By the time we got there, Jim was unconscious and on a respirator.

The doctors whisked us to a waiting room and asked the minister to follow them. I was alone. I prayed with few words.

Joanna, our minister, returned muttering, "We arrogant sighted people! I told them they should have talked to you first, not to me!"

Jim's doctor slipped in, quietly answering my question about our wedding on Saturday.

"I'm sorry, Lauren, but there may not be a wedding."

I nearly fainted.

Jim's electrolytes were fatally out of whack. He was not expected to live. I would not become Jim's wife, after all.

Joanna tried to comfort me by saying that we were already married in our hearts; all we really needed was her signature on a piece of paper, and she would do that no matter how things worked out with Jim's health.

Somehow I made it through the night. When I called the hospital the next day to arrange a time to visit Jim, I was suddenly met with colossal apprehension—"Maybe it would be easier for you not to come. Maybe it would be better for Jim if you stay home. We don't want to take any risks," the nurses advised.

Marilyn and I knew exactly what this was about, and as we walked in, she gave the nurse on call an unforgettable rendition of how I was nearly Jim's wife, and, blind or not, I needed to be given every consideration and treated just as respectfully as if I could see.

Jim was sedated so he wouldn't expend extra energy, but they awakened him so we could attempt to communicate via finger movements. Since we had never communicated finger-wise previously, Jim drew letters in my hand, on the bed, and finally on a piece of paper on which a nurse could read his scribbling.

"Call Mom," he said. His mom had been there four days but Jim didn't remember.

Jim had developed pneumonia and a badly infected gallbladder with stones. He was too ill for surgery, but they were able to insert a drain to help heal the infection until he was strong enough to have the gallbladder removed. Miraculously, his health began to improve immediately.

It was still touch and go, but we prayed every day. My prayers felt flimsy to me, but our minister's beautiful singing went straight to Jim's heart.

When our choir left a message on the phone, Jim listened, smiling!

On the twenty-fourth, our original wedding date, I sadly joined my family at Memorial Park, thinking about all the families who lost someone and how they had to carry on. Would I have to do that, too?

Two days later, I received a very strange phone call. It sounded like an old man on the other end with a very hoarse voice. I couldn't understand what he was saying and almost hung up. Then he said, "And I love you." It was my Jim!

At the hospital, we no longer communicated finger-wise—we talked.

Thursday, we made the decision to hold our wedding in the hospital. Jim made arrangements on his end. As none of his immediate family was able to be present, Jim chose the very same doctor who had told me several days earlier there may not be a wedding to be his best man!

Friday morning I frantically called for flowers, food, and a cake. Baker's Grocery had everything ready that evening.

Our makeshift wedding was complete with Marilyn singing "The Rose" and several choir members singing to us, my parents, my sister and her family, friends of ours, and, in the back of the room in jeans, hiding—my daughter, Lynden.

Jim, who "got out of having to wear his tux," and I were married by our minister, and then we shared our blessing with hospital staff by inviting them to have food with us immediately following the ceremony.

Although the doctors felt several years ago Jim was living on borrowed time, Jim and I celebrated our third anniversary on May 30, 2000.

Somehow, Jim and I have connected since day one on a level far beyond the physical. If we consciously thought about the "what ifs" (as many around us have done), we would never have met, let alone lived!

Many have questioned why I would marry someone with such a medical background, and others may wonder why he would marry me, since I have several disabilities besides blindness.

Perhaps it is because we love one another.

—LAUREN MERRYFIELD

Lauren and her husband, Jim, recently settled into their own home surrounded by trees in Mill Creek, Washington. They live with their two feline "boys," Jaspur and Mikey. Their daughter, Lynden, is attending college in Nebraska, the family's original residence. Thanks to Heartwarmers/Petwarmers, Lauren is not only writing, but becoming quite an Internet surfer using her screen-reader software, JAWS (Job Access With Speech). She has done telemarketing and hopes to find gainful employment in a more honest and purposeful environment.

The Spirit of Santa Claus

EARLY IN 1998 MY BELOVED DADDY HAD TO BE PLACED IN A NURSING home. Alzheimer's disease was stealing away his memories and his abilities to function on his own. I was heartbroken—I knew it was the end of the daddy that I'd known. I couldn't conceive of him not being there for me like he'd always been. He was so cheerful and happy and always had a "Howdy!" and a kind word for everyone he met.

He had been doing fairly well for the past few years but was failing daily. All of us were used to hearing the same stories repeated many times and laughing at the same jokes. We became accustomed to skillfully losing at the card games he so enjoyed playing. Seeing him slowly slipping was so sad.

In early April, Daddy became seriously ill and was rushed to the emergency room. He never came home again. At age 87, many of the usual medications were too strong for him, and his body and mind could not tolerate them. He slid the rest of the way into

Alzheimer's unreality, although there were days when he seemed to be "normal."

Even though the staff at the nursing home was kind and treated him very well, he always asked Mom when he was going to be well enough to go home.

He watched for her to come every day. She kept him occupied during her visits with short walks around the center and with word search puzzles and a golf putting game. It broke her heart when he'd repeatedly ask to come home. She kept telling him that he was ill and that whenever he no longer required medicine, he could come home from the hospital. He would frown and get sad, but would acquiesce.

When I could come to see him, we'd race with the puzzles to see who could find the most words. I, of course, let him win a good majority of the time. Daddy was no longer a vital adult male; he was a young boy again in his mind. I'd frequently leave the nursing home in tears.

But Daddy wouldn't have wanted it that way, if he had known. Daddy was always a cheerful spirit who never knew a stranger. He talked to everyone he met and had hundreds of friends. The first time he was ill, several years previously, he received over 95 cards and letters from folks in the community just because the local newspaper had printed a notice that he was in the hospital.

His motto for his produce and real estate business was "Howard Wants to See You!" and he was truly happy to see anyone who came into "Howard's Produce," his place of business. When he was first in the nursing home, since he felt pretty good, he would "help" the nurses out by pushing their medicine carts for them or by pushing the wheelchairs of those more restricted than he. He always had a smile and a "Howdy!" and most would respond with great cheer, "Howdy, Howard!"

When my parents first moved to Florida, Daddy had for many years played Santa Claus during the holidays at various shopping centers. He loved to watch the eyes of the kids as they met Santa and told him about their desires for presents. As I live in Orlando, where Walt Disney World is located, I found a Santa hat with Mickey Mouse ears that I brought to Daddy his last Christmas.

He was thrilled! Even though Alzheimer's was messing with his mind, he immediately remembered that he was Santa! He insisted that Mom help him on with his red flannel shirt, put on the hat, and said, "I've got to go entertain the girls!" He then shuffled out to the nurses' station on his wing. He grinned at them and proceeded to do a little jig—he captivated the whole group! In fact, they were so enthralled they even took pictures!

For Mom and me it was a sad caricature of what he had once been. But to see the joy it brought him, and the staff and patients all around him, was heartwarming.

In late February, when it became clear that Daddy was to be with us just a little bit longer, word quickly spread around the nursing home. During the three days before he passed away, every nurse and aide in the home who had ever cared for him came to his room to say goodbye. One by one they stopped in for a minute, patted his hand, paused, and then left.

The morning he died, the charge nurse for his unit actually left the home and drove to our house to tell us Daddy was gone, as our telephone had been busy for an extended period of time. She hugged Mom and cried with us as if it had been her father who had passed away.

We held a memorial service for Daddy several days later, after his cremation. We knew that there would be a huge outpouring of friends and associates at the service. Daddy touched so many lives during his lifetime. But what said even more about the kind of man he was, and the people who loved him, was the attendance of Daddy's favorite nurse and aide. Daddy even opened the hearts of those people who take care of patients like him every day, staff unlikely to attend the funeral of an 88-year-old patient who has passed along.

We brought Daddy's ashes to be buried in his home in northern Missouri. Five minutes before the ceremony was to begin, the heavens opened and a torrential rain began to fall. We straggled into the cemetery under recalcitrant umbrellas, wishing it could be different. At precisely 2 P.M., however, just as his funeral service began, the rain ceased and the sun smiled through the clouds. We all laughed and said, "Howard's at his magic again! He must have asked God for some sunshine for his homecoming—that would be just like him!"

Daddy left sunshine everywhere he went, even the nursing home where he resided for his last year of life. The spirit of giving and helping others never left my daddy while he was alive. I doubt anything is different now that his home is with God. He's probably still doing his magic tricks and playing Santa Claus.

—DEB HAGGERTY

Shirley Ogle, Deb's mother and Howard's widow, lives in St. Petersburg, Florida, is an artist at counted cross-stitch, and enjoys crossword puzzles and e-mailing friends and relatives. Deb Haggerty is an author, consultant, and speaker who lives in Orlando, Florida, with her husband, Roy.

$\mathcal{L}$ife Is a Bucket Truck

My husband of 35 years, Worth (short for Hollingsworth), asked me to go with him to pick up a truck located way out in the country. He didn't know if he had fixed it well enough to get it back to his auto parts store, and he wanted me to follow . . . just in case.

The fixing part and the just-in-case part should have clued me in that we were in for another one of Worth's outlandish episodes—we have had many in our long marriage!

We got to the truck; I about fell out when I saw the thing. It was a dilapidated, corroded, crappy-looking bucket truck that had to have been resurrected from a long-ago junkyard. And I thought, "What on earth is that man going to do next!"

I did appreciate Worth's mechanical and driving abilities, which are nothing short of brilliant. He can make a vehicle do anything and go where it has never gone before. He even raced on the NASCAR circuit with Richard Petty, although I honestly don't think Petty has ever maneuvered like Worth.

After much ignition-throttle cranking, producing sputters and spitters, I was thanking the Lord the truck wasn't going to start. I was praying that Worth would give up on his foolish idea, and we could return home.

But my prayers were not answered. Or maybe they were—with a resounding, "No, I won't make Worth give up!"

It started up, in a loud, unearthly way, shattering the serene country landscape. The chickens in the poultry building nearby probably had heart failure from the noise, or suffocated from the smoke the beastly machine was putting out. At the very least they would be some pitiful-looking jaybirds, after all their feathers flapped off.

So off we went. It was right out of a down-yonder redneck movie. Picture the scene: The fastest the bucket truck can go is 25 mph. I have to keep my windows up because of the choking fumes from the extended trail of smoke. Did I mention it's 95 degrees out and I have no air conditioning in my car?

Worth isn't exactly driving straight because the steering on the thing isn't working just right. One of its tires is looking about as flat as a cow pile, and the side utility doors are banging open and shut because they're too decrepit to just stay shut. It's obvious none of the people in the line of traffic collecting behind me are going to venture a pass. Goodness knows the language that was flying out of their mouths that morning as they cursed this old fool ahead of them.

I am thinking, "When I dreamed what life would be like, this wasn't exactly it!"

We're going up a long hill, and the bucket truck is trying to muster up enough power to make it to the top. Twenty-five mph keeps dropping . . . and dropping . . . until standstill. Then it starts rolling backward slowly, then a little faster. And it's not looking good at all.

I stop my vehicle, put on the emergency lights to warn the people behind me, pray about what I should do next, and . . . well, I just pray. I'm about to get creamed by a bucket truck. I consider leaping out of my car to avoid certain death, when suddenly, I do not know how, the beast moves forward again to the top of the hill, and we continue on our journey home.

Now we're on a flat stretch of road with pastureland on both sides; and we come with loud noise and thick smoke. Cows to the left and cows to the right all scatter to the back of the pastures as fast as they can go. Have you ever seen a whole mess of cows running? Usually they are just munching on grass and lying around. The noise and thick black smoke were too much even for them. They're running into each other and for their lives.

We get to the main highway and by now the bucket truck is smoking worse than ever—the other drivers behind me must have been totally frustrated at best, probably infuriated.

Finally, after 30 minutes, which felt like hours, we reach the store. Worth rolls the truck into the parking lot to a grand-finale stop. I am now sitting in the pickup truck totally speechless. I still haven't figured out what we're going to use this monstrosity for, and at the moment, I don't really care.

Worth casually walks over to me, grinning, and in his amusing way says, "Once or twice I didn't think I was going to make it."

Worth never does these rash things just to do them. They're not rash to him—he always has a reason.

We don't talk about the bucket truck the rest of the day. I'm afraid to even raise the subject. I go about my business, for the thousandth time in my marriage, shaking my head in wonder at this man I married.

The next day I see for myself the purpose of the bucket truck. I walk outside to see my husband, Worth, raised in the air in the bucket (which does work), placing a huge store sign that says "MAC'S AUTO PARTS" on a very tall pole.

At this moment, Worth is a happy man. He's in his 70s, and he's still doing things himself and saving money to boot.

When Worth was a police investigator, he caught many a criminal with his off-the-beaten-path methods . . . quite by surprise I might add. We have had many adventures in our home, each one coming with Worth's intrigue and ingenuity, mixed with his subtle humor and my frank astonishment.

I have often asked, "Lord, why me?" The answer always seems to be the same: because Worth is a good man, and because I love him so much. Besides, somebody's got to do the praying.

Because life with Worth is just one bucket truck after another.

—GLORIA McMILLION

 Gloria and Worth live in Amelia, Virginia. They are semiretired and have two grown sons. Gloria was a registered nurse and over the years has dabbled in photography and writing. Living with Worth, needless to say, has been and continues to be an interesting life.

The Day My Heart Was Kissed

WHEN I WAS SIX YEARS OLD, I RECEIVED A KISS THAT WAS SO PROFOUND, it left an everlasting impression and literally changed my life.

In the summer of 1970, I lived on Main Street in Westbrook, Maine, with my parents, my three-year-old brother, and my one-year-old baby sister. We lived in a three-bedroom apartment building on the first floor.

My parents had a lot in common with each other. Both were the eldest of three children in their families. They both lost their fathers to cancer at a very young age, and they both grew up in emotionless homes. No one ever said "I love you" or gave hugs and kisses in their families.

Unfortunately, that same coldness and lack of intimacy got passed down to my siblings and me. It was a lonely and sad home within which to live.

I was a quiet, yet inquisitive child who was considered a loner. I was rather average, the type of child that never made an impression one way or the other. I was so envious of the children in the park whose moms and dads hugged them and kissed them and made them feel loved. I imagined what it would be like to feel so cherished. I just sort of blended into the background, a fill-in for the surroundings of life.

Kindergarten was a frightening experience for me. I went to school in the basement of Saint Mary's Catholic Church, located a few buildings down from our house. I walked to school by myself, passing through a field behind our house and then cutting through the park, then into the building. Inside, the church smelled musty, and hordes of nuns were walking around.

I had never seen a nun before in my life until I started kindergarten. I didn't know what they were until I got older. All I knew then was that they were quiet and they dressed funny.

Although I tried making conversations and was kind and friendly, I was not accepted by my peers. My mother once chastised me for giving away my belongings to try to gain friendship. Needless to say, they took my possessions while I gained nothing but heartache. It was a desperate time for me.

One hot, muggy morning I was walking to school. I was wearing a summer dress that hung on my scrawny frame, with my waist-length blond hair carelessly tied in a jumbled ponytail. My shiny, black buckled shoes were glimmering in the bright sunshine. As I was walking through the green, grassy field, I heard some type of construction going on in the distance. I then cut through the park and had to stop.

The church parking lot had huge, deep holes dug into the asphalt. The ground was littered with gigantic concrete cylinders, and the air smelled of smoldering tar. There were several workmen doing various kinds of work, wearing jeans, work boots, tank tops, and hard hats. I stood at the edge of the asphalt and froze in terror.

My mind was spinning like a top. "How could I get to school? Should I go back home? Should I go back and play in the park until school gets out?" I feared punishment if Mom and Dad found out, but I had no idea how to proceed.

Just as my throat was closing and I was getting ready to cry, one of the workmen came over to me and with a southern accent said words I still remember to this day: "My, my, my! What's a purty little girl doin in a place like this?"

Purty little girl? No one had ever called me pretty before.

I was astonished.

He politely tipped his hard hat. "Ma'am, may I?" And then this kind stranger gently picked me up, carried me across the parking lot, and tenderly put me down in front of the church door. I was already in disbelief, but his final moment with me is what changed my life.

He took a battered-looking bandanna from his pocket, dusted off my black buckle shoes, and said, "Can't muss up them purty little shoes, now can we?"

And then he kissed me. Right on the forehead. He smiled at me, and then walked back to his work.

It would be a long time until I could fully concentrate on anything. My heart was soaring! Someone cared about me! He said I was pretty! Then I must be!

Every day that I walked to school, I looked for the kindhearted stranger. Unfortunately, I never saw him again.

He probably has no idea how he changed my entire outlook on life that day. It dawned on me: If a total stranger could touch his lips to my forehead and not cringe in disgust, then maybe I wasn't so bad after all.

I gained confidence in myself. I could go to school with my head held high. I began to make friends.

It was more than a kiss that he gave me that day, or even a helping hand across the parking lot. He gave me my self-esteem back. He helped me love myself by reminding me that I was beautiful.

—PENNY FROST

Penny Frost is a freelance writer from Lewiston, Maine, who enjoys reading, writing, and spending time with her husband and six children. She tells her husband and children that she loves them every day. They are all very close and affectionate. Outside of the home, she always sticks up for the underdog and she maintains close contact with distant and not so distant relatives. Penny reports that after 30 years, her family couldn't be closer. "My children have the best grandparents and I have two best friends."

Stepmom's Reward

MY STEPDAUGHTER, AMBER, HAS LIVED WITH HER DADDY AND ME FOR five years. She is a second grader and visits her biological mother every other weekend. Although we have gone through many struggles, I feel we have a pretty good relationship. She even calls me Mommy. Since she was three years old, we have had to go through many changes and adjustments and continue to go through them today.

I've been told oftentimes that my reward as a stepmom will come in Amber's adult life. When she's old enough to look back on the things I've taught her, given her, and shared with her. I got a glimpse of that reward in McDonald's.

We had been out shopping on a Friday afternoon before Amber went to her mother's for the weekend. We stopped in a McDonald's so that she could change clothes and my one-year-old daughter, Lauren, could snack on some French fries.

During the course of our visit, we were "entertained" by a mommy, a daddy, and a son going through a family struggle that we, unfortunately, were witnessing.

Daddy was leaving the McDonald's with the young son in his arms. Mommy ran after them while the boy cried for Mommy, and she pulled at him. They stopped just in the doorway. After both of them struggled for him, the boy finally went to Mommy with an exchange of several words between Mommy and Daddy. A few short minutes later, Daddy returned to give Mommy the boy's medicine. He sat it down on the trash bin just inside the door and left. Mommy, while holding the boy, then ran out to Daddy's car, where, I'm sure, more words were exchanged.

The restaurant seemed to stand still watching this episode unfold. Mommy eventually came back into the restaurant and asked to use the phone. She called the police.

During this whole scenario, I began to narrate to Amber what I thought was happening. I told her that the son's parents had probably just gotten a divorce. I told her how difficult it must be for the son. He loves his mommy and daddy very much and wants to spend time with both of them. And he's probably torn between going with his daddy and staying with his mommy.

I told Amber I felt sorry for the boy because he had to hear the shouting and feel the embarrassment of being in a public place for everyone to hear.

I tried to explain to her what life must be like for the son.

At that time, Amber looked at me and said, "If my mommy and daddy got divorced, I'd want to live with my mommy."

I was shocked. We had gone through a situation recently where Amber told us she wanted to live with her mom. I thought we had gotten past that.

So, I asked, "Is that what you really want? To live with your mom?"

I guess she saw the look of disbelief in my eyes, and said, "No, if you and Daddy got divorced, I would want to stay with you!"

Tears welled up in my eyes in amazement. I told her that was a very sweet thing to say and that I hoped that it was a decision she'd never have to make.

Wow! My stepdaughter would choose me over her own daddy! All the times I'd yelled at her to clean her room, pick up her stuff, take a bath, do her homework. She loved me after all! Really loved *me!*

All of the struggles of the last five years were worth it, to experience that moment in McDonald's.

Being a stepmother requires wiping away tears from a little girl who misses her "mom" and wondering to yourself if she misses you that way, too. It means wondering if the card she made in school on Mother's Day is for you or her "real mom." It spawns some funny moments when you and "Mom" are in the same room and your stepdaughter yells "Mom!" from the other room and both of you answer at the same time.

It requires a lot of love to raise another woman's child. But when that child loves you back, it's not so impossible after all.

—KAREN DAY

Karen Day lives in Elizabethtown, Kentucky, with husband, Rick; daughters, Amber and Lauren; and two cats, Bonnie and Clyde. Not only have she and Amber gone through struggles, but there have also been struggles with other family members during the adjustment of step-parenting. Karen loves being a mom whether it's step or biological. She works full-time in the school system and loves spending time with family.

A Nickel's Worth

WHAT A SCARED LITTLE SEVEN-YEAR-OLD BOY I WAS WHEN THE orphanage finally let me out of that dark closet, after two days of being trapped inside. I took my bath, brushed my teeth with soap, and dressed myself for school in the clothes that the matron had laid on my bed.

When I reached Spring Park Elementary I just kept on walking past the school building. I was afraid that the other kids in my classroom were going to make fun of me because of all the black-and-blue marks that were on my legs, where I had been whipped with the polo paddle.

I walked and walked for what seemed to be hours. Finally I came to this great big wide street at the end of Spring Park Road. I had never seen a street that big before, or so many cars in all my life.

Across the street was a big brick store, and the sign on top said "Preston's Drugs." There was also a sign in the window that read, "Everything you'll ever want is here."

It took me almost an hour to get across Atlantic Boulevard because I was so scared of the fast-moving traffic. Finally, I ran across the road as fast as my legs would carry me. I walked into the large Preston Drug Store and noticed people sitting at a counter drinking drinks with ice cream in them. I had never had ice cream before. But that is not what I was looking for anyway.

The sign said "Everything you'll ever want is here." I wanted something very special. I set out to find it.

I looked, and I looked, and I looked, but I just could not find the thing that I had heard about on the television movie. Suddenly an old man grabbed me by the arm, scaring me half to death.

"What are you doing in here, boy?" he yelled at me.

"I'm looking for something special," I told him, as I backed against the wall.

"Are you stealing stuff?" he yelled again, as he poked me in the nose.

"No sir, mister," I whimpered. "I'm not a stealer."

He took me to his office, and a policeman came by and asked me why I was not in school. I didn't tell him anything because I was afraid that he would take me to jail for running away from the orphanage. So I just started crying real loud.

The policeman couldn't get anything coherent out of me, so he left the office and sent in to talk with me a pretty lady, about twenty-five years old, who came in and sat by me. She was the woman who was working behind the counter serving ice cream and drinks when I arrived in the store.

"Where do you live?" she asked me. "Were you stealing?" she wanted to know.

"No ma'am. I live in that big orphanage on Spring Park Road. I came here looking for something special," I told her.

"And what might that be?" she asked.

"Do you have someone to hug kids in this here big store?" I said to her. "I just want a hug."

"We always have hugs for kids in this store," she assured me. She stood up, wrapped her arms around me, and squeezed me real tight.

As far back as I can remember, it was the first hug I had ever received in my young life. Even now, 47 years later, I still remember it as if it just happened.

Then she smiled at me and walked real fast out of the small office, with her hand over her mouth. I looked out the office door and saw that the back door of the store was now open, giving me easy exit out of the store. I quickly walked out of the back door and I ran all the way back to school.

I went without milk at lunch that day. That's because I laid my nickel on the desk at the Preston Drug Store, to pay for the hug that nice lady gave me.

It really was "the store that had everything in the world that you would ever need," and I didn't steal it either.

—ROGER DEAN KISER, SR.

Roger reports that one of the best hugs he's ever had in his life was as an adult, attending the first Heartwarmers Convention at Niagara on the Lake, in Ontario, Canada. He received it from Lee Simonson, Heartwarmers founder, after a heartwarming speech that didn't leave a dry eye in the place.

Goodbye, My Love

IN NOVEMBER OF 1999, MY FATHER, JACOB, DIED OF A STROKE. THIS wonderful man was a gift, so his passing during the season of Thanksgiving was most appropriate. In all those years, he was a good husband and father, so losing him was hard. But at the age of 90, he earned and deserved a long-awaited rest.

Jacob was a loving, gentle man. He and my mother brought six children into the world. Our mother died young, and Dad remarried a wonderful lady named Laura. They spent 30 years together, after he had spent 30 years with our mom.

During the last years of his marriage to Laura, he cared for her every day as she suffered from the devastating effect of Alzheimer's disease. For the last year of his life, he was living in an assisted living apartment, with Laura in another facility on the grounds where she could receive 24-hour nursing care.

Laura became childlike and frightened of even the smallest things. But one thing always cheered her—Dad's daily visits. They would walk hand in hand around the grounds and up and down the halls, happy to be together, and as much in love as they were the day they married. It upset her greatly when he would leave, because she could not go with him.

In her world, there was nothing wrong with her. Being the good wife that she always was, she could not understand why she could not go home and "take care of the house and her husband." This was very hard on Jacob. On many occasions, I saw the tears roll down his cheeks as he left and went back to his apartment alone.

During this time, Jacob had a stroke and his end was nearing. We talked to Laura's doctor about how to handle Dad's death with her. Would she understand? How would she react? The doctor suggested that we not tell her about Dad's death, as she would not remember being told anyway. The doctor felt that if we mentioned his condition, it would cause her new pain and stress. We decided to tell her that Dad was sick and would not be visiting for awhile. Eventually, we thought, she would forget.

One of Dad's biggest worries in life was that his beautiful Laura would not be cared for properly, with love, when he died. We assured him that we would take care of her, and he did not have to worry about her. Although he was in a coma, he seemed to hear us and rested much easier after he heard these words.

When we knew that Jacob's death was near, we changed our minds and brought Laura to the hospital to visit him. We knew this is what he would have wanted. Some of the family worried that Laura would not understand, and worse, that she would become upset. Others of us felt it was important for them to say goodbye. Let her think it was only a visit to a sick man, we decided.

As Laura came into Jacob's hospital room, she looked at him and asked, "Who is this man?" We told her it was Jake. She moved closer to the bed. Then she walked to the head of the bed and looked into his face.

Jacob was still in the coma and his eyes were closed. We believed that if there was one shred of life left in this man, he would know that Laura was standing next to him.

Gently, Laura brought her hand up to his face. She stroked it very lightly, smoothed down his hair, and quietly and lovingly looked into his face for the longest few moments that I could ever remember living through.

Without words this dear old couple was saying goodbye. He in the coma, and her in the world of lost memories.

Did they connect? Yes, we are sure they did. Love travels in ways that we will never understand, on paths that only the Lord can explain.

Dad lived for five days after Laura visited him. We took him off all forms of life support, according to his wishes, and we moved him to my sister's home so that we could be with him during his last days.

With the help of a wonderful hospice group, we made Dad comfortable in the middle of my sister's living room. Her entire home became a place of prayer, song, visitation, and last farewells. Each person from the eldest to the smallest greatgrandchild, had the opportunity to hug, stroke, and kiss Grampa Jake goodbye. We sang every old song he and Mom ever taught us (and there were many), we held hands around his bed and prayed for the family, and we gave him messages to deliver to our Mother and brother.

When the moment came for him to leave us, it was a peaceful passing.

Laura remains in a beautiful nursing home, with her many loving family members visiting her daily. Laura's room is filled with pictures and cards to keep her connected to her past. There is a lovely picture of Dad and her among these mementos. Does she feel sadness and pain when she looks at these items? I don't think so. She seems content. Many times she will talk about her husband. Is she referring to Jacob? Who knows? She was married to another man for 30 years before my father.

Memory plays strange tricks on Alzheimer's patients, but seems kind to her. Perhaps this sad disease has released her from the mourning we all feel. That would be a kindness that she well deserves.

I see Dad in Laura when we are together. It is hard to know where one began and the other ended. They were a unit. A visit to Laura is like visiting with Dad.

Holding Laura close when we visit not only fulfills the promise we made to Dad before he died, it also reconnects us to him. Loving Laura, or "Grandma Laura" as she is to the children, is an extension of loving the Dad and Grandpa we so miss. They were inseparable in life, and to us, they are still together.

—ROSEMARY SALZMAN

RoseMary continues to write about the things that are most dear to her. She and her husband, Philip, enjoy living in the beautiful countryside of central Wisconsin, in a 116-year-old, one-roomed refurbished schoolhouse. They are avid readers and have filled their "house of learning" with their wonderful collection of books. RoseMary takes joy in the nature around her and her old schoolyard with its grand old oaks and many new shrubs, trees, and flowers they have planted. She also enjoys hiking, card making, crafts, golf, the Green Bay Packers, and her warm and wonderful country neighbors.

RoseMary and Philip have three grown sons and three lovely granddaughters, who are the loves of their lives!

*D*ream Dancer

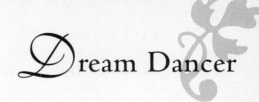

I AM A DANCER. NOT IN TALENT OR BY TRADE, BUT THROUGH EVERY fiber of my heart and soul.

I am also a newlywed.

So, where's the connection? Since my earliest memories I have always dreamed of one day donning an incredibly romantic gown and waltzing around a dance floor draped across the arms of my Prince Charming. Now I know it's hard to believe that a woman of 47 years could aspire to such an unfeministlike fantasy. But despite a lifetime of feminist consciousness-raising sessions and ERA bra burnings, my dancing dream has somehow just never faded away.

So, last year, when Michael, the man of my dreams, finally got up the nerve to pop the question, unbeknownst to him, the dance portion of our wedding had already been predetermined. I had a dream, and in it Michael and I were Fred and Ginger incarnate!

Although as I stated, I am a dancer, I must be honest. I've never had a lesson in my life. However, anytime I gyrate around my bedroom to "Living La Vida Loca," I am absolutely fabulous! I have also been known to outdance all challengers at the "two for one" margarita nights held in my hometown. So my part in our bridal dance recital was sure to be a snap.

Michael, however, was another story.

He is, by trade, a home remodeling/construction engineer. Michael can walk across a 6-inch beam, 20 feet in the air, without a second thought. But put him on a dance floor without the beneficial reinforcement of a few beers, and his coordination bravado turns to mush. He was a dance-floor emergency screaming for choreographic CPR.

Fortunately, this wonderful man understood the dance demon within my soul.

He was also more than familiar with my strong-willed Irish determination. So when I suggested a few sessions of ballroom dancing, he reluctantly cast his feet to the wind.

First, we chose our music—a romantic Irving Berlin standard entitled, "Always," vocals by a very young Frank Sinatra. It was dreamy and slow, and I was on cloud nine. I could feel the realization of my dance dream drawing ever near.

Then we actually started to dance.

Lesson one amazingly went quite well. We mastered the basic waltz steps in quick order. Halfway through our instructional hour we were even twirling and turning. I was impressed and somewhat amazed by Michael's Astaire-like instinct. Perhaps we actually would achieve wedded waltzing bliss. We concluded our first tutorial with the instructor's admonition to go home and practice, practice, practice.

Unfortunately, by the time we finished our exhausting daily list of chores in preparation for our nuptials (which were held in our home), we were neither physically, nor mentally, capable of toe tapping anywhere but directly to bed.

I started to get nervous.

Actually, bitchy would probably be a more accurate term. I began having nightmares about dancing disasters, starring me as the embarrassed performer. In response, I devised a plan. There might not be time to practice, but we could still make this waltz work. All I had to do was choreograph a dance that we could memorize. Once we had it entrenched in our brains, the actual performance would be a piece of cake!

Now this seems like an appropriate moment to mention that Michael is a man of infinite patience, great endurance, and best of all, endless love for me. When he listened to my dance plan of salvation, accompanied by two pages of arrows and footed diagrams, he simply smiled and said, "I'll give it a try."

I laid out the patterned steps and we practiced—first without music and then with it. After five or six tries we were doing pretty well. I was sure we were going to WOW the instructor with our choreographed prowess.

A week later in dance class, as we stumbled and sputtered through each step, we took our rightful place in the "dancing fools" hall of fame. We were a disaster. The instructor stopped the music and directed us to return to the basics. Within a few minutes, we were once again waltzing with ease. With the responsibility of leading once again returned to him, Michael capably took charge and I grudgingly tried to follow.

As the music wound down, the instructor suggested a gentle dip as the pièce de résistance to our production. Michael masterfully supported and guided me backward, and I dutifully followed . . . almost. I suddenly jerked up. I couldn't do it. I was sure I was going to fall.

The instructor stopped the music and straightforwardly stated, "You don't trust him. You're afraid he won't hold on to you. You do the same thing when you're dancing. You try to lead because you think he won't."

I was stunned by her comment and, moreover, embarrassed by its accuracy. I managed to stumble through the remainder of our lesson, then rode home without saying a word. I went straight to bed but spent most of the night tossing and turning while reviewing my life in random order. I slowly began to realize that virtually every difficulty I had ever experienced related to a basic lack of trust. Not only of others, but also of myself.

I was shocked, almost numb. I lay in the darkness and wondered, How did such a simple thing as a dance lesson point out such a basic insecurity in my being? Was it possible that at this stage in my life I could change? More importantly, if trust is the basis of any successful relationship, could I truly commit to marriage with this wonderful man that I so dearly loved?

I awoke the next morning and asked Michael if in the two weeks left before our wedding we could make the effort to get up 20 minutes early and practice. As always, he smiled and said, "Sure." We began that morning.

We chose to dance on the front porch with the garden as our backdrop. As the musical introduction began, I took a deep breath. I tried to let my inner reflexes relax; my defenses drop.

For the first time in my life, I actually allowed someone else to lead me.

At first, I felt like a wooden soldier: stiff and unnatural. This wasn't just hard, it was impossible! I wanted to quit! But something about the kindness in Michael's eyes kept me within his arms.

We started the music over, and then again and again. Was it my imagination, or were we actually dancing? Never having truly danced before, I was unsure.

But whatever we were doing, I was starting to enjoy it.

Each morning we dutifully met on the porch. It didn't matter who else was in the house or what tasks needed to be done. We both stayed true to our practice commitment.

On our wedding eve morn, madness prevailed. Routine did not. I panicked, sure that without that crucial final practice we were doomed to fail. Michael turned his loving blue eyes to mine and calmly said, "We'll be fine. Trust me."

Little did he know how much he was asking.

Our wedding day dawned gloriously and unfolded to perfection. It was the dream of a lifetime, complete with a beautiful heirloom dress and a handsome prince charming. After our vows were spoken and the celebration began, the first strains of "Always" drifted across the tent. I gingerly placed my hand in Michael's as he led me through our first dance steps as husband and wife.

I moved stiffly at first, then increasingly more pliantly, bending and swaying to the wonderful waltzing rhythm. Suddenly, Michael raised his hand and twirled me in a circle. My fancy dress gown swirled around my ankles and it felt just as I had always imagined it would.

I began a giggle that rolled into laughter and dissolved into tears. I was living the dream of my lifetime and it wasn't just about wearing a girly dress and waltzing. It was about being loved, and loving enough in return to trust.

As young Frankie's crooning tones began to fade, Michael gently braced my back and gracefully dipped my body.

And this time, I let him.

I am truly a dancer.

—CHRISTINA M. ABT

Christina M. Abt is a freelance writer, enjoying life with her husband, Michael, in their 150-year-old upstate New York farmhouse where they breed championship Morgan horses. She is a newspaper columnist, a guest commentator for her local NPR radio station, and a national magazine feature writer. She is also a two-time contributor to the first Heartwarmers *book ("Just Wanted to Talk" and "Gino's Kindness"). She is the mother of two awesome children and will always be her mother's daughter.*

$\mathscr{M}$idsummer Night Dreams

THE SUMMER I WAS 10 I SPENT AT MY GRANDMOTHER'S HOUSE. SHE lived in a very small, dying town in the Midwest that had once been bustling with life.

Giant steel mills had employed thousands, but slowly the mills were closing and the population wandering away to find work in other places. My grandmother's house was a 22-room mansion built by a colonel who had led a division of the Pennsylvania Militia in the Civil War. The foundation was carved from giant blocks of granite, four by four by eight.

There was a cupola on top where only the bats went now, but there had been a time when the colonel's wife had spent each day there, waiting to see her husband and the men in his command come back to their homes from the last battle in Virginia.

The summers were filled with endless time for long walks along the remnants of a side branch of the old Erie Canal, which followed behind my grandmother's property. And there was time for baseball played on the sandlot next to John Jackson's tinsmith shop.

After the games, Jackson would take the team up to his wonderful wooden-floored building and let us help him solder handmade oilcans for the railroads. They were the famous Jackson Oilers, long-spouted copper cans his father had invented, which had helped change a horse-and-buggy country into a transcontinental wonder. We were thrilled to know that the cans we worked on would be oiling steam engines across the country.

He let us scratch our initials on the bottom.

At night, when trains roared through town, the baseball team would sometimes wake from their sleep and wonder if the giants they heard were purring softly, their wheels moving smoothly, thanks to a Jackson Oiler they had made.

My favorite times were the long summer evenings spent in the wide rocker that hung from the ceiling on the big front porch. No one could see us sitting there. The trees that arched over the long slate walks to the street shadowed the porch. "Ma," as I called Grandma, and I would sit until well past my winter bedtime, telling stories and laughing, watching fireflies and conspiring against the adults.

My mother wasn't one for hugging, and her two sisters seemed distant and cold. None of them remembered ever being hugged by Ma. Ma told me my mother and my aunts were so different from her that she sometimes couldn't believe they belonged to her. I decided that it was because they had been born in winter while Ma and I were summer children, our birthdays only eight days apart.

I had been named for my grandmother, which meant that I was, in some way, her. She hugged me, not only with her arms and the warm softness of her ample body, but with the intimacies of her life that she confided to me.

I was so proud to be entrusted with her secrets and the most cherished memories of her more than 80 years.

On one such evening, I asked her the story of the ruby-and-pearl lavaliere that never left her neck. She pulled me closer to her on the swing, her arm encircling my shoulders, her breast warm and soft against my cheek through the fine cotton of her dress. She didn't answer for some time.

She was gone for a moment, lost in the sweetness of the past. One time she had told me that "sometimes the only vacation spot left is the past."

Finally she began to talk.

"Your grandfather gave it to me the week I turned forty years old. He'd given me a surprise party with all my family and his, and friends from all over the farm country, but after the party I was sad. I was growing older.

"I wasn't a girl any more. I was no longer young. There was gray in my hair, and though I'd just given birth the year before to your mother and would mother your Aunt Mary ten years later, I thought I was getting too old. I'd always had a good figure, but it was sinking fast. It took me longer to do some of the things I had

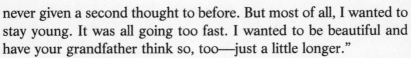

never given a second thought to before. But most of all, I wanted to stay young. It was all going too fast. I wanted to be beautiful and have your grandfather think so, too—just a little longer."

I asked if she had told Grandfather how she felt. She said that she had not, that she would have been embarrassed, particularly after the lovely party, and the flowers he had bought her, and the other things he had given her. No, she had kept her sadness to herself.

The next evening she had gone to church to help with the arrangements for Sunday school. When she came home, up the same slate walk we were looking at now, Grandfather had been sitting on this same swing, waiting for her.

He didn't speak but took her hand and led her inside to their bedroom.

There, on the bed, was a little black velvet box. In it was her lavaliere, along with a note. He was not a man of many words, she said, but she would never forget these:

To my beloved on the occasion of her fortieth birthday:
The first time I saw you, twenty-two years ago, I fell in love
*   with you.*
All these years I have respected you and loved you. You are
*   so beautiful.*
I just want you to know that my legs still go weak when I
*   see you. And, when you let your hair down and come*

to me, sometimes I think I'm going to faint. This little gift will remind you of that whenever you wear it, and of how much I love you.

She held me close to her for a very long time, lost again in that bedroom with my grandfather. I didn't speak for fear of ending the moment.

Finally I fell asleep. I had no idea how long she stayed, but now I suspect she spent that entire summer night with him.

—NANCY REUSCHER

Nancy Reuscher is a resident of Sausalito, California, and writes novels, short stories, and poetry. Her family is the source of much of her writing.

Her grandmother, about whom she has written here, taught her the most important lesson of her life. As she lay dying at age 86, Ma whispered to her 10-year-old granddaughter, "I want to tell you something really important. The most important thing I can give you. Remember it! When you get where I am, years and years from now, know how you got here! Take responsibility for your life and your actions. You are what you make of your life. Make it what you will, but 'own' it at the end. Mistakes and successes. No matter what happens—know how you got here!"

*H*eaven-sent Blessing

I WAS DEFINITELY "DADDY'S LITTLE GIRL," AND THIS WAS NOT INFLU-
enced by age, either. No matter where I went or what I did through
my life, I knew and felt Daddy's love and protection.

This loving relationship also made it easier to accept the con-
cept of a loving heavenly father.

During the late 1980s, both Mom's and Dad's health started
failing, and they had to live in a care center. Daddy was diagnosed
with Alzheimer's, which shocked Mother and I, as he had always
been so vibrant and active. He was a professional singer in his
younger years and still loved music. When I came to visit him, I
would sing a song for him, and he would start singing along with
me, remembering all of the lyrics. Even though he wasn't always
quite sure who I was, his eyes were smiling. No matter what happened to his mind, our spirits were always connected.

It was around Thanksgiving of 1991, and I was living in
Arizona at the time. I talked to Daddy on the telephone and wished

him a Happy Thanksgiving. He knew who I was as we talked. I said, "Daddy, I'm sorry we can't be together this Thanksgiving, but maybe next year."

He said, "No, honey, I won't be here next year."

A chill ran up my spine as he said that, almost like a confirmation of his premonition.

The call came, December 10, 1991, from the Las Vegas care center. It was my mother tearfully relaying that Daddy had passed away. Not my wonderful, sweet, precious daddy who I felt would always be here! The days following were managed only through the grace of God. That's when I learned about what "Amazing Grace" really means.

Days, weeks, and months passed, as I worked through my grief. The pain lessened and tender memories flooded the emptiness inside my heart.

I started attending a little local community church and found the people to be warm, honest, and only too glad to welcome me to their fold. Day by day, my inner strength grew and life didn't seem as bleak as it had. On Wednesday nights, Bible study groups (called JOY Groups) were held in different people's homes. One evening, my intuition strongly told me to attend one that was only a few blocks from where I was living. I followed the hunch. When I arrived, there were about 10 or so people from the church. The leader, Ray, welcomed me. It turned out to be more than a pleasant evening. It was a new beginning in my life.

Ray impressed me as a very nice, distinguished, caring individual. He was carrying a very strong burden (his wife was dying of cancer and was in the final stages), yet he still managed to care deeply about the spiritual welfare of those who came in contact with him. He had been in a grieving process for quite some time now, taking care of his wife during her final days and without relief.

A lady from the church, Irene, and I became very good friends, and I moved into an apartment right across from hers. My eighteen-year-old son decided to cut the apron strings and move to his own apartment. With my son gone, and my daddy passed away, it was a new time of aloneness for me. These were soul-searching days for me, a time of renewal and restoration. It was also a time of friendship. Some evenings when I returned from work, there would be a small knock at my door, and it would be Irene, bringing me a hot plate of some delicious creation she had made for dinner.

I felt as though I had extra angels surrounding me all the time, and Daddy's presence, to help supernaturally heal my wounded heart and revive my joy. Ray was also experiencing a similar time, as his wife passed away a few months after I met him. We had become good friends and my heart was hurting for him in his loss.

Time passed, and then one day, after church, Ray asked if I would like to go out to lunch. I enjoyed our friendship, so I agreed.

We went to a quiet, quaint little Chinese restaurant. Over a simple lunch, Ray expressed a romantic interest in me that went beyond the casual friendship I thought we had.

This thought had not previously entered my mind.

At first, it was awkward making conversation. I felt like a tongue-tied teenager. Eating lost all appeal. He then said, "I didn't know if you would be willing to go out with an older man."

I asked, chuckling inside, "How old do you think I am?"

"In your late thirties?" he queried cautiously.

I laughed and he gave me a puzzled look. He was probably afraid he'd really blown it and insulted me.

I then asked his age, and he said he was 54. I smiled, took a deep breath, and said, "Ray, I'm fifty-two!" We both had a good laugh, and the ice was broken.

How could I turn down a man who thought I was 15 years younger?

This began a new time of getting to know each other as more than casual friends. A few weeks later, Ray went to Oregon to visit relatives. He and his brother drove together into Montana and back through Washington State.

During this drive, Ray tried several times to call me on a cell phone. He finally got through, and when I answered, I almost dropped the phone.

He said, "Do you think you'd like to marry me?"

I had come to love and respect this man, and so with my heart in my throat, I shouted, "YES!"

Before we married, I wanted to get the blessings of my parents for our wedding. I was very sad that my daddy would never know Ray. I know they would have liked each other very much. Even at my age, in my 50s, I yearned for my Daddy's approval of the man I planned to spend the rest of my life with.

We decided to travel to the care center in Las Vegas where my mother still resided, to celebrate her seventy-ninth birthday with her. She was clearly happy for me, and I felt more complete having brought Ray and my mother together.

Still, as we drove away, I felt an incompletion because we couldn't share this happiness with Daddy.

God works in mysterious ways, and on our long drive back to Arizona, I got exactly what I was praying for. There was a lull in our conversation, each of us lost in our own thoughts. Then Ray slowly said, "God just spoke to me." He said, "She is yours forever, my son, for I have given her to you."

I started to cry tears of joy as I exclaimed, "*I got my wish!* My father in heaven and my heavenly Father are giving me away!" My daddy had given me the blessing that I needed before marrying Ray.

I was finally at peace.

We were married on October 3, 1993. I walked down the aisle with my daddy in my heart, instead of standing at my elbow. And it was okay. I knew he was there. I have no doubt that my daddy watched every minute of the ceremony, smiling from heaven.

—JOYCE CAROL STOBBE

 Joyce now lives with her husband and Sheltie pet in the tall pines of Oregon, in a little house on a mountain. She enjoys being a retired homemaker, author, composer, in spite of her daily battle with fibromyalgia and Chronic Fatigue Immune Dysfunction Syndrome. Her strong faith in God supplies the needed strength to take and enjoy one day at a time.

$\mathcal{U}$nlikely Friends

"HI MA," I HEARD ON THE OTHER END OF THE PHONE. ALTHOUGH HIS voice now contained an accent, and I hadn't heard from him in three years, I knew immediately who it was. After all, Louis was the only person who called me "Ma," a nickname he had given me eight years ago in high school. Our relationship was shaky back then. I disliked Louis from the start.

He was tall with a large and muscular physique, and on many days wore his favorite color, camouflage. So when he spoke to me one day, I admit that I was frightened of his deep voice and rough tone. Louis didn't seem to have a sensitive side to his demeanor.

"Are you his mother?" he asked me when I was telling a fellow classmate what to do. I wasn't sure what to say to him since I didn't really know him and never thought I'd want to. So I responded with a snide remark and hoped that he would mind his own business. That didn't happen. He had broken the ice between the two of us with his continued charade of teasing me.

I found it odd that he was talking to me at all. From what I observed, he didn't seem to be much of a conversationalist. But something must have opened up inside of him that day. This quiet, keep-to-himself kind of person didn't keep to himself any longer. At least not where I was concerned.

Louis would constantly call me Ma. He would never let me live down the fact that I had been bossy, and he had witnessed it. He would pick on me any chance he got with this smirk on his face that I will never forget. And that smirk would only grow as I got more angry.

So how did our long-lasting friendship begin? There was no precise moment; it was more of an evolution. I remember beginning to laugh with him, to hold conversations that no longer just held jokes aimed at me. I began to see the kind, gentle side of him, even though he tried to cover it up the best he could. I found myself looking forward to class with him. The teasing stopped, and, at last, we were both on the same side, rooting for each other instead of competing.

Somehow it happened—Louis had touched my heart, and I guess, although he never verbalized it to me directly (you know how these macho guys are), I had touched his heart as well. That year in class, a friendship blossomed, one that would be stronger than I ever thought possible.

When I watched Louis step forward at graduation to get his diploma, I wiped a tear away, fearing that I would not see him anymore. I had come from despising him to considering him one of the most important people in my life. How did that happen? Life is mysterious sometimes.

Now, I wondered whether a friendship as unlikely as ours would disintegrate once we no longer saw each other in school every day. Would we keep in touch? Would our friendship fade? I gave him a congratulatory hug as he told me how wonderful it was to be "outta here." I could only stand back and watch, imagining what it felt like. I still had two more years to go.

That summer, I met up with him several times as I walked by his house on my daily exercise excursions. When I had to train for cross country, he graciously offered to go running with me. Each time we got together, we said goodbye with a hug. One thing I'll always remember about him is the way he made me feel about myself. If I said something bad about the way I looked or how poor I was at something, he would find the good in it and yell at me for thinking anything different. He fed me compliments and made me feel beautiful at a time in life when I needed to hear it. Isn't that ironic, given that our relationship started with an insult.

When he went off to live in a dorm at college, we spent hours on the phone with each other. He helped make my writing more descriptive as I worked on my weekly English assignment. I'd brag to him about the many A's I'd received, because he loved knowing how he'd helped me achieve them.

"I'm joining the navy, Ma," he announced to me one summer afternoon. It was a statement I had always expected from him. His dream had always been to become a Navy Seal. I knew that he would eventually make it his career. I just didn't know it would come so soon. I was forced to say goodbye, knowing that I would rarely, if ever, see him again.

While Louis was stationed in Pensacola, Florida, we exchanged letters regularly. Sometimes, four months passed without my hearing from him. When I finally received his letter, he would apologize profusely for taking so long to write. After he was shipped to Japan, his letters became more and more infrequent.

I arrived home one day to find a message from Louis saying that he was home and that he would like me to attend his wedding the next day. Wedding?! I was surprised to hear from him and startled to hear about his wedding plans.

But I was so happy for him. You bet I'd be there!

I remember thinking, as I walked into the church and saw him, "He hasn't changed a bit." I stood there watching him get ready for his big moment. I was looking at the same old Louis. And when we shared our familiar hug, I felt as if we hadn't been apart at all.

But watching his bride walk down the aisle and say "I do" made it that much clearer. He had been gone. He was creating a life for himself that I knew virtually nothing about. That knowledge left me feeling a bit melancholy.

We were drifting apart, and yet, still, mysteriously, always together.

I took pictures of his wedding and cherished the time I was able to see him. A short hour later, he was on a plane to his honeymoon, and then on to his new life in Japan.

I continued to write to him at his new address, but I wasn't getting any response. To put my mind to rest, I sent him a letter via certified mail. I got the return receipt with his signature on it. But alas, no letter from him was forthcoming. My many letters went unanswered, and, finally, after more than two years of trying, one of the letters came back stamped "no longer at this address."

I can't say for sure why I didn't phone his mother to inquire about him. Probably because I was hurt and angry, as I was the only one making the effort to stay in touch. That was my way of getting back at him, I suppose.

Still, I felt an emptiness in my heart without contact with my friend Louis. Somehow, I just couldn't, or wouldn't, let it go so easily.

Heartbroken, I finally put my words in a story and sent a note to his mom asking that she forward it to him.

"My mom sent me a story you wrote," he told me on the phone, almost three months after I'd sent the story off to his mom. He apologized, explaining that his job kept him away from home for six-month stretches and that left him with little time to write.

"Thanks for reminding me how important it is to keep in touch with the people I care about," he shared.

I hung up the phone that night with a smile on my face. Our friendship had survived! I felt at peace, and complete, for the first time in a long time.

I often think back to the days when I despised Louis. I am so thankful that he kept teasing me long enough so that I eventually let my guard down and began to laugh with him.

He was right about me—I can be bossy at times. Especially when I feel really passionate about something or someone. It's a good thing for him, and for us, that I wasn't about to let this friendship fade away into oblivion. He can call me Ma all he wants. It's music to my ears when he says it.

—LYNN M. LOMBARD

Lynn and Louis are now communicating more regularly by e-mail. Louis promises that he will call from time to time. She no longer worries about losing their friendship. She believes they are bonded together in friendship forever. She looks forward to seeing him in person again, someday, and hopefully getting to know his new wife as well.

$\mathcal{B}$order Crossing

My girlfriend, Anne, and I had rented a car in Canada and were heading south, toward the state of Florida, to get married. As we were traveling through Montana, several unmarked police cars stopped us and began to search through our things. They told us that they were searching for guns, which I found rather hard to believe as they were going through all my legal documents and reading my personal letters.

I mean, how many handguns did they think a person could stuff inside a regular-size letter envelope?

About the time they were going to allow us to continue on our trip, one of the police officers noticed that I was an American and that Anne was a Canadian. We were immediately arrested and taken to the jailhouse in Great Falls, Montana, where we were questioned for several hours. They said something about someone with a car like ours running guns in that area.

I was finally released and told that I could leave and continue on my journey to Florida. I asked about Anne, and they told me that she would be taken back to Canada, in several hours, and handed over to the authorities. Anne did not have the proper visa to be living in the United States.

I thought I would die right there and then, on that very spot. There was no way that I was going to leave Anne behind, no matter what I had to do. I mean, I would have done anything to get her back. I followed the police car to the Canadian border at Sweetgrass, Montana, where they allowed me to kiss Anne before they took her away. I told her that I loved her more than anything in the world and that I would do whatever it took to get us back together. I told her to get a room at the hotel, on the Canadian side, and to call me at the pay phone, at the border station, as soon as she got settled in.

I waited for her call, and, sure enough, she called me two hours later.

Over the next two days I talked with Anne on the telephone my every waking moment and told her that I was trying to arrange a marriage ceremony, which would take place at the border crossing.

The next day I found out, from the state authorities, that this could not be arranged and that there was no one who could legally help me, because it was a federal issue, not a state one. I decided right there and then that I was going to take matters into my own hands.

I was 24 years old, and maybe I was naïve. I could not get it through my head why a man and a woman who lived on the same earth, and who loved one another, could not be together. Because some idiot had drawn invisible lines on the face of the earth that told people that they must stop right here, on this very spot, and not take another step?

I was going to get my Anne, no matter what.

I noticed that in the evenings there was only one guard on the Canadian side and that the American guard went home. As I stood there, late one evening, looking across at the Canadian side, a very nice looking girl came up to me and asked me if I was looking for a date. I told her that I was but that it would be with the girl I was going to marry.

I remembered seeing this same girl talking with the Canadian and American guards the day before. When she realized that she was wasting her time with me, she said goodbye and walked away.

"Hey, wait a minute," I yelled at her.

She turned around and said, "Well, big boy, that was a fast change of heart."

"No, that is not what I want," I told her. I asked her how well she knew the Canadian guard that was working the Coutts Alberta guard crossing. She told me that he was a nice guy but that he was always trying to get her to give him "special favors" for free. I explained my situation to her and asked her what she would charge me to get him out of the small building just long enough for me to get Anne across to the American side of the border.

She told me that it would cost me $50. I told her that I would give her $25 now and the other $25 after I got Anne across the border. It would be the best 50 bucks I ever spent.

I watched as she talked, laughed, and joked with the Canadian guard for over an hour. She finally turned him around with his back toward me, and I ran across the border, heading toward the small hotel where Anne was staying.

When I knocked on Anne's motel room door, she opened it and her eyes got real big and pretty, and I could tell that she was surprised to see me. She smiled real big, and then she ran up and kissed me as hard as she could.

I told her to grab her things as fast as she could and that we had to hurry and get across the border. When we got back to the border crossing, the guard was nowhere to be seen. Anne and I ran to my motel and gathered my things and packed them into the car. Then Anne went back up to the room to use the bathroom. As I turned around I saw the girl standing there with a strange look on her face.

"Going to skip out on me?" she accused.

"I would not do that," I assured her. I reached into my pocket and counted out $25 and handed it to her. She took the money and then reached into her purse and took out the other $25 that I had given her. She placed all the bills together and rolled them up into a small roll, then handed them back to me.

"What is this?" I asked.

"I just wanted to make sure that you were not a liar," she said, before turning around and walking away.

After traveling about 20 feet she stopped, turned back around, and said, "By any chance, do you have a brother?"

"I don't have anybody, except Anne," I said.

"My name's Betty Boo and I don't have anybody either," she said, rather softly. She lowered her eyes toward the ground, smiled faintly at me, and turned back around. I saw her wipe her eyes on a dirty tissue as she slowly shuffled away into the evening.

I hope she found somebody to love her, the way that I found Anne.

Anne and I piled into my car and headed to Florida. We had a wedding to attend.

—ROGER DEAN KISER, SR.

Roger's book Orphan, *a very moving account of Roger's life in an abusive orphanage, was released in December, 2000. His poignant messages are sharp, sad, heartfelt, and sometimes humorous. Roger hopes his book will be read by all who truly love children.*

*A*nthony's Wish

ANTHONY WAS 21 WHEN HE RECEIVED HIS HIGH SCHOOL DIPLOMA before a standing ovation. He was a spirited member of the class of 1981—my graduating class.

The story goes that when Anthony was in his early teens, joyriding with his friends was cut short when a train slammed into them. As a result, Anthony had to relearn the basic mechanics of life and spend the rest of his schooling days in special ed.

"J-Jen-uh-fer," he stuttered to me one day in our senior year. He was breathless with excitement. "I-I'm h-having a birthday party! W-will you come to my p-party?"

I glanced at his birthday invitation. A clown danced on the face of it, and pencil-smudged letters were scrawled childlike on the reverse side. The party was scheduled during the deepest part of summer, well after graduation.

I hoped that my smile camouflaged the doubt taking root. I couldn't say no to him, as he went on, beaming, "I-I'm having lots of f-food and soda pop and-and a dis-co-teque!"

"That sounds great, Anthony!" I replied. "Sure, I'll come," I assured him, mustering up as much enthusiasm as I could portray. "Tell me what you would like for your birthday."

He named an album by a popular rock group and handed me another invitation to give to my girlfriend. That night I slipped his invitation under a magnet on our refrigerator door.

For weeks thereafter, all the way up until graduation night, Anthony reminded me of his impending birthday party. But when summer tempted me with other plans, I must admit that the invitation soon sunk to the bottom of my priorities. However, my conscience begged me to do otherwise. I couldn't forget Anthony's face when he implored me to come to his party.

My friend Lexie and I went Dutch on the album that Anthony requested, and on that hot, dry midsummer day, we landed on the doorstep of his tiny house, which was strangely quiet. Our knocking summoned, surprise of surprises, the homecoming queen from our high school. She appeared relieved at the sight of us, since she had been the first to arrive.

The house did not exactly look ready for the party of the century. It was dark from drawn curtains, and a floor fan oscillated fruitlessly in the withering heat. The size of the living room made me wonder if the DJ was going to set up the discotheque in the backyard. It was then I noticed an old turntable with albums stacked next to it. This was to be our "discotheque."

On the coffee table was the homecoming queen's gift to Anthony—obviously an album. I set ours on top of hers. The dining room table boasted two plastic bottles of warm soda, and between plates of towering, triangular-cut sandwiches was a homemade layer cake. No one had bothered to inscribe a birthday wish in the chocolate icing. Anthony's mother had left town for the weekend.

Anthony appeared out of the gloom with his trademark crooked smile, dressed in his best casual suit and platform shoes, which boosted his height to well over six feet.

Another knock at the door. A popular cheerleader stood there with some uncertainty, a gift-wrapped album under her arm.

A pattern soon emerged with each subsequent knock at the door. Before long, the house overflowed with beautiful girls piling albums on the coffee table. We shook our heads in amusement. Anthony would have been the envy of every guy in our high school.

We flung open the curtains and windows to release stale air and shed light on the party. The sandwiches, left out overnight by Anthony, were supplemented, through a quick stop at the store from volunteers, with chips and dips, more sodas, and a chest full of ice. Twenty-two candles were erected in the icing of the birthday cake.

Someone cranked up the "discotheque," and at the birthday boy's request, each of us lined up to take turns slow dancing with him. When it was my turn, I tapped the girl on the shoulder and said, "Hey, you're hogging him up!" Anthony was clearly tickled by this.

While in his stiff embrace, my hands clasped behind his neck, I smiled broadly at my partner, who was a million miles away. I was tempted to offer him a penny for his thoughts. But glancing at the long line behind me, I figured I better not get him rambling. As the others had done before me, I planted a firm kiss on his cheek before giving him up.

I will never forget the faraway expression on Anthony's face that summer day of 1981, his cheeks smeared with frosted shades of lipstick from birthday kisses. When he paused before blowing out the candles, his dazed eyes reflected the fervent wish of every teenager. He had experienced the immeasurable joy of fitting in. On this day, he was one of the popular kids at school.

While attending college, I received sporadic phone calls from Anthony, who had moved with his mother to Reno and found a job at Circus-Circus. On our last conversation, he asked if it was all right to send me a letter. I said, sure.

Two days later, I opened an oversized FedEx envelope and groped around inside it until I found a piece of ruled paper folded into a square. His familiar handwriting read:

> Dear Jenifer,
> How are you? I am fine. I like working at circus circus. Can I send you a stuffed animal for your

birthday? I hope you are well. When is your birthday?
Please write me.

> Your friend,
> Anthony

I wrote him back but never heard from him again. I have often wondered since then about whether he found someone to love, and a girl to love him, whether the joy of that day carried him forward in life. I often replay the dance I had with him, when gazing into his distracted, clear eyes I felt a kinship there. Our minds may not have been on the same level to a degree. But our hearts were.

Anthony, wherever you are, may your victory ring out the rest of your days.

—JENNIFER OLIVER

Jennifer is a computer specialist with the federal government in the heart of Texas. She and her husband, Stephen, enjoy raising their four kids out in the country, and when they're not working on their fixer-upper, their passion for antiquing and visiting small towns consumes their weekends.

Safehaven

WHEN I WAS A LITTLE GIRL, THERE WAS ONE PLACE I KNEW I COULD always go to be safe. That place was in the massive, burly arms of my father. Whenever I was sick or troubled and had difficulty falling asleep, my dad would lie next to me and envelop me in his loving embrace. He would draw my small body next to his gigantic frame, and my fears would magically fade away. I instantly melted into the warm folds of his arms and contently floated off into the splendid delights of dreamland.

When I was about 12 years old, there arrived an evening when I wasn't feeling very well. I desperately needed to get a decent night's sleep but instead, tossed and turned in a state of restless frenzy. Hoping to soothe my anxiety, my dad unselfishly offered to cuddle me until I drifted off to sleep. Being a teenager, newly determined to assert my independence, I rejected his suggestion and chose instead to bury my face in a neglected book.

Later that night, I quietly stumbled out of bed to go to the bathroom. I overheard a discussion in which my parents were engaged. My father, with a quivering voice, was crying to my mother that his sweet, precious angel was growing up, and she didn't need him as much as she used to. He confided to my mother how desperately he wanted to preserve me at an age of innocence from the harsh realities of the world. He expressed such love for me, and such pain, I could barely fathom it at my young age.

I silently crept back to the darkness of my bedroom and pondered over the reasons for my father's dismay. What on God's Earth did I do that caused my dad to cry? I crawled into bed and tightly wrapped the velvety blankets around my body. As my head met my pillow, I was reminded of the afternoon my father taught me how to ride a bicycle.

He was clutching the back of my bike as I nervously pedaled down the narrow, sandy alleyway behind our modest home. I made him solemnly promise that he wouldn't let go of my bike until I told him I was ready. I'm sure his eyes gleamed with proud tears as he watched me slowly wobble my bicycle away from his protective grasp.

At that moment, as I lay awake in my bed, with my melancholy father down the hall, I suddenly realized that it was probably more difficult for my father to let go of my bike than it was for me to tell him to do so.

I reflected on the look of rejection that washed over my father's face that night as I swiftly dismissed his suggestion to comfort me. At that very moment, I understood why my father was so sad. By telling my dad I no longer needed him to help me fall asleep, I had unwittingly taken another step on a long road toward adulthood. I had advanced on the path of autonomy, anxious to navigate my way along the winding trail of life that lay before me. I stepped out of the safety net of my father's arms, brave and eager to encounter the adventures and heartaches that awaited me.

What my father didn't realize then is that there was one thing of which I remained certain. If the world of independence upon which I was embarking contained more hurdles than I was prepared to jump, I always had a safe haven in the tender arms of my father. I knew his arms would forever be available to applaud my achievements and guide me through the course of my life. I felt confident to welcome my newly discovered maturity because I was positive that as challenges flew my way, my father would always know when it was the right time to extend his arms and hold me ever so tightly . . . and when it was time to set me free.

My father may have thought that I was rejecting his efforts to comfort me. What was really true, was that I had grown old enough to make the choice of when and how I relied on him, and sometimes, I had to do it on my own. But as I have grown up, my father's love and protection has always been with me, and always will be.

Even when he's not there to wrap his arms around me, I carry him with me in my heart.

—KAREN KREUZER

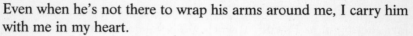 *Karen Kreuzer is currently a single mother of a beautiful 12-year-old girl, Raeanna. She works full-time at a law firm while attending college on a part-time basis. She has always enjoyed writing and plans to take some writing courses in the near future. Her father has recently retired from the U.S. Postal Service. Her mother says that even though she is now an adult and living on her own, she is still her father's "baby" and she holds the key to his heart.*

$\mathcal{O}$ne Last Gift

ONCE UPON A TIME IN THE LITTLE TOWN OF HAVANA, THERE LIVED A white-headed, soft-skinned, kindhearted countrywoman known as Grandma Quinsey.

Grandma Quinsey, who was my father's mother, never had the need to be anyone other than herself. Unlike most people in the world, Grandma Quinsey never wanted to modernize in any way. When my daddy and Uncle Joe moved her into an updated home that had "hot water heater capability," she wouldn't let them hook it up. She told them "she would rather heat her wash water on the stove and carry it to the bath tub." She made them take out that "new fangled" electric stove and hook up her old, trustworthy "Baby" (an old iron woodstove). She had cooked on that old stove for six children and knew just exactly how to regulate the temperature on her "Baby."

I had the honor as a child to stay with Grandma Quinsey after school as I was growing up. I could hardly wait for the school bus to stop rolling before I would take off at a run to see what Grandma

Quinsey had for me in "Baby's warming ovens." I'd try to guess as I ran whether it would be fried chicken, buttermilk biscuits, sliced taters, crisp bacon, or my favorite of hers, "Chicken 'n dumplings." I was never disappointed or hungry after I got there. As special treats, she might have hidden some "ice tray ice cream" or "syrup taffy." I loved pulling the handle on the old-fashioned ice trays to release the cubed ice cream—another one of her non-modern methods! Boy was it good!

My Grandma Quinsey grew up working. Because of that she never really had a chance to be truly "educated." It broke my heart the first time that I realized she could only write her name and could not read very well. In school, I was quite an accomplished speller—thanks to Grandma Quinsey. I loved to enter the spelling bees, and Grandma Quinsey would help me study. She would say the letters out loud, I would pronounce it for her, she would say it, and then I would spell it! Maybe in a little girl's mind, I was trying to help her by getting her to help me. I did win county two years straight—and boy was Grandma Quinsey proud. I told her I could never have done it without her.

Grandma Quinsey and my Uncle Herbert (who had a speech/hearing problem) became my neighbors after I grew up and married. Grandma Quinsey believed in paying her way. She didn't want you to do anything for her unless you let her pay you in return. After many arguments about how I *was not* taking any money for whatever I had done for her, we came to a satisfactory mutual agreement. When she felt like she owed me, she could feel free to have me over for a bowl of steaming hot chicken 'n dumplings for supper. And she would. I really think I got the best end of that deal!

One of my daughter's second-grade projects was to interview her oldest living relative. Guess who—it was Grandma Quinsey, who was then 89. We kept putting off this interview—we were so busy—running to one ball game, horse show, school event or another. Finally on Sunday, May 7, with video recorder in my hands and the list of questions she planned to ask in Nicole's hands, we closed the distance between our homes for the necessary interview.

The day was gorgeous. The sky was clear blue, the temperature was mild—we should be at the beach somewhere, we were thinking. Oh well, first let's just get the school assignment over with, we grumbled. Grandma Quinsey met us outside, and Nicole and Grandma took their positions in the old straight-backed porch chairs.

I started the videotape rolling as my daughter fired off her questions. "Where were you born?" "What was your childhood like?" "Were you happy?" "Were times hard?" "What were your clothes like?" "What did you do for fun?" "What type of beauty products did you use?" "Did ya'll get to have parties?"

Grandma Quinsey replied, "I was born in Fitzgerald, Georgia. I started working young in life to help make money to help my daddy support the family. I started plowing with a mule when I was about your age. If a girl ever gets to plow one time—you'll be hooked and want to do it again. I was very happy even though food was scarce and the unnecessaries were not even thought of. I was so excited when my sisters outgrew their clothes and I would get them. I used to get to play hide 'n go seek, and hopscotch with my sisters. I really didn't have much extra for makeup and besides my daddy wouldn't let me wear that stuff. A woman who wore too much makeup and lipstick when I was growing up was not called a lady. We would have ice cream socials and tin can parties. At the tin can parties, everyone would take the label off of their cans and put them in a box. Each person would get to pick one can out and that would be their supper for the night."

I sat in silence as I captured the minutes on tape. As Nicole's interview ended, I kept the tape rolling and continued asking Grandma Quinsey questions that popped into my head as we talked. My Grandma Quinsey, who was usually short with her information, was a motormouth. She even gave me her prized chicken 'n dumplings recipe. As the day came to an end, I gave Grandma Quinsey a hug and thanked her for taking the time to answer our questions. As I always did when we parted ways, I told her I loved her.

I threw the video camera with the tape inside back up on the shelf when I got home. I was tired and housework was waiting! The next morning I woke up about 4:30 A.M. and couldn't sleep. I was out of the shower and dressed when at 5:15 A.M. my phone rang. When I said hello, I heard the struggled words of my Uncle Herbert, "Come on! Mama sick!"

I threw the phone down, screamed at my husband, and ran out the door in the dark of early morning toward my grandma. My heart and mind were racing. I entered her room, calling "Grandma" as I did. She was lying on the bed and turned her head toward me as I entered. I said, "Grandma, what's wrong?"

Tears streamed from my eyes as she tried to smile at me and answer me and nothing came from a mouth that only moved on one side. I immediately called for help. I sat stroking the hands that had so often lovingly rubbed my back for me. I sat smiling and reassuring her when I felt like tearing the door off the hinges. No! It couldn't be! Not now.

The ambulance arrived, and as daybreak graced the eastern sky, my grandma breathed in the sight of one more day. At the hospital, the doctors shared that my grandma had suffered a cerebral hemorrhage that was so extensive that nothing could be done. They assured us that she was not in pain—it could be hours or a day— but Grandma Quinsey was not going to make it.

I was not ready to say goodbye. I sat stunned as I thought of how many times in the last month we had put off going to do the videotape interview. God knew—He allowed us to have one last gift from Grandma Quinsey. He gave us a tape full of Grandma and memories that because of our "don't have the time," "we'll do it tomorrow," "I'm too tired," we almost never got to have.

As painful as it was, I forced myself back into Grandma's room. I was scared—I wanted to run away as far as I could—but I couldn't leave Grandma Quinsey alone; she would never have deserted me. The heart monitor revealed that her heart was still beating. The nurse shared that even though Grandma Quinsey couldn't talk to us, the last thing to go on a person is his or her hearing.

I became a motormouth. I told Grandma how much she had meant in our lives, how I hoped to one day be able to always find the good in people like she did, how much we would miss her on Earth but would see her again, how we would take care of Herbert and not to worry about him.

As I ran out of words to say, one single tear slipped out of the corner of my grandma's eye. My sister wiped it away, and we both leaned down to kiss our grandma one last time. As we stood up, the heart monitor straight lined. The only words I spoke as we once again parted ways were, "I love you, Grandma."

—GLENDA Q. SHEPARD

 Glenda lives in the country with her husband and two teenage daughters. She feels that the most precious gifts are the ones God has given or those given from the heart.

$\mathcal{A}$ Sister's Love

I STOOD THERE LISTENING TO THE STERN WORDS OF MY FATHER.

He had gathered us into our enclosed patio and had the look on his face that told us all that one of us had done something wrong.

"Which one of you did this?" he asked with a sharp voice.

We all stared down at the floor containing the art of a child's handwriting in chalk. I suppose that had been a no-no for us, though I can't say I remembered that part when I was committing this horrible crime.

I stood there, trembling on the inside and hoping that no one else could see it. "Will he know it was me?" I fretted. Too scared of the consequences of telling the truth, the only words that came from my mouth were, "Not me, Dad."

The others denied it as well. Of course, we knew that one of us must have done it. But I, being the youngest and smallest of the three, just couldn't find the courage to tell the truth.

It wasn't that I was a bad kid. Lying was not normal behavior for me. But the look on my dad's face that evening sent a chill up and down my spine.

I couldn't bring myself to tell him the truth.

My dad had a way about him when I was a child that made me afraid of him. But I loved him for it, too, because it gave me limits and boundaries. I wanted to please him—so much, that I decided to hold back the truth that day. I couldn't let down the one man I looked up to.

Without saying a word, he disappeared for only minutes and came back with a piece of paper and a pencil. He was so determined to find the culprit!

"I want each of you to write exactly what you see on the step," he ordered sternly.

I was not a stupid kid. When my turn came, I deliberately wrote the words differently. So when my dad compared the handwriting, he still couldn't tell which one of us had done it.

Frustrated, he stood a step above us and peered down at his three small kids.

"I'm going to give you one more chance to confess," he admonished.

He continued to stand there for a few moments, but to me it seemed like only a second. Not surprisingly, neither my brother nor my sister spoke up. Why should they? I was the one who had done it. Should I say something? Was it too late? Every time I almost got up the courage, I talked myself out of it. He'll be mad! So again, frightened, I held my tongue.

"Well, if someone would have come forward when I asked, there would have been no punishment."

"Oh, no! I've lost my chance! Now it's too late. Stupid, stupid, stupid! I should have confessed! Now I'm gonna get it!" I berated myself.

He took us all into the house as tears welled up in my eyes.

"Since none of you seemed to have done it, then you all get a spanking," he declared.

Still, I stood there and said nothing. The last thing I wanted was a spanking! I didn't know what to do.

"I did it," someone said, and I was pretty sure it wasn't me.

I looked around to see my sister, Sue, come forward.

Huh? She did it? No, she didn't. I did! Why was she was taking the blame for something I did?

Feeling guilty, yet still scared to 'fess up, I stood there knowing my sister was going to get spanked for something I did.

Perhaps if this were a Disney movie or a children's story, this is the scene or chapter where I would leap forward with my confession, preventing my sister from taking the heat for my actions.

But this wasn't a movie or a fictional story. And I didn't have the courage. I let it happen. She got spanked because I didn't speak up.

My sister and I didn't talk about that day for many years. We were teenagers by then. Sitting around the living room talking about days long past, I pondered out loud the time when this happened. Knowing that now that we were all older, it was safe to tell my dad it was really me, I finally confessed. I remember him looking at me with wide eyes and a dropped mouth, "And you let your sister take the blame for you?" he said, half-kidding. "I didn't spank her hard anyway," he laughed.

My sister, Sue, didn't seem surprised at all by my confession. Of course she had always known it was either my brother or me. She wasn't upset with me. She simply kidded me about it and still does.

Sue was my protector, my worrywart, and my best friend. She still is. That day, which now seems so long ago, she would have rather taken the pain herself, than see me suffer. She would do anything for me. I'm glad to say that as I've grown up, I can say without hesitation, that I would do the same for her.

—LYNN LOMBARD

 Lynn and Susan have continued to have a special relationship. They remain very close, meeting for lunch once a week and talking on the telephone regularly. They were each other's maid of honor when they got married and know they are bonded for life.

Tablecloth Stains

"I WAS FOUR FOR A SECOND, BUT NOW I AM FIVE," MY FRIEND CATHIE'S five-year-old told a new friend a few days after his fifth birthday.

Those words express the feelings of so many parents, especially at this time of year. We had a wide-eyed baby for a second. We blinked and had a little girl who wanted to be a princess when she grew up. Faster than the wave of a wand, our princess was a student and a tennis player and, oh my, she walked into the gymnasium last night with her high school classmates, wearing a mortarboard.

On the morning after our daughter's graduation and her subsequent graduation party, I'm up early, gingerly walking on a kitchen floor sticky with cake crumbs and bits of frosting. Trash bags are overflowing. But the serving platters are washed and surrounded by several unopened presents. I see the beginnings of her thank-you list on the kitchen table.

Typical of my sweet, loving daughter, after I had collapsed into bed, she had worked late, trying to put some semblance of order into a house that showed all the aftereffects of celebration. But even she had her limits, and the job wasn't quite done.

I turn toward the dining room. I wince—not because of the crumpled blue and gold napkins and a few dirty plates—but because I see a kitchen towel attempting to blot a seeping red punch stain on my beige lace tablecloth.

My heart sinks. Will I ever be able to use my favorite tablecloth again? I regret the loss.

But then I found another way to look at that stain, and it comforted me. Years from now, when my daughter would probably be long gone out of our home, it would be a reminder of a very happy night, a time when the house was bursting with proud adults and lively kids. It would remind me of the sound of her laughter and the joyous look on her face. This tablecloth stain was just one of many ways that she had left her mark on the world, on my world.

Every bit of common sense urges me to hurry, get that tablecloth soaking. Maybe if I get to it in time, we can use the tablecloth again at Thanksgiving and Christmas.

Carefully, I lift the tablecloth from its hanging place and take it upstairs to soak it with Biz, the way my mother-in-law taught me. While making suds my mind begins to reminisce about all the other cherished items I have saved, stains, blemishes, and all.

I gave away most of the party perfect dresses and suits that no longer fit the children. But I have saved threadbare blankets and favorite T-shirts and sundresses. The books I treasure most are the ones with tattered pages and worn-out spines. The three dolls I tucked away look ready for toy heaven.

The rest of the family sleeps while the tablecloth soaks and I write. We have two graduates and two more to come. Time is going fast. I can't stop the clock, but I can put my thoughts on paper so that these moments don't slip away forever.

After about an hour I check the tablecloth. The red is fading. In fact, it is almost gone. It looks like the tablecloth will be perfect again. As I gently stretch the fabric and lay it out to dry, I see no evidence of punch, no sign of a party in the intricate lace design.

I am strangely sad to see it go.

When I take the tablecloth out next Thanksgiving, I'll search again for the stain's dim outline. And I will hope to see it there.

—GRACE WITWER HOUSHOLDER

 Grace Witwer Housholder is a Heartwarmer Gem and the author of "When A Camper Gets No Mail" in the first Heartwarmers *book. She is a journalist and author based in Kendallville, Indiana. The mother of four, her books are* The Funny Things Kids Say *and* Quotable Kids—Fun in the Family Tree. *She is the founder of The Funny Kids Project (www.funnykids.com).*

$\mathscr{N}$ever Forgotten

WHEN PEOPLE ASK HOW I FIRST BECAME INTERESTED IN SIGN LANGUAGE, I hardly know how to answer. I didn't have deaf parents or a little deaf neighbor who wanted to play with me. But, from my childhood, the yearning to know sign language was deep and demanding. Later, when as an adult I learned to love the Welsh poet Dylan Thomas, I found a way to describe part of my early attraction to sign language.

Thomas once said that he "loved words, the very taste of them"; at some deep place in my being, I shared that love. Words have always been my hobby, my passion, and I understand very well how Dylan Thomas could love the "taste" of them, because I do, too. When I discovered sign language, I came face to face with a new idea—words whose beauty was not in their "taste," but in their rich visual textures and patterns.

I learned a little sign language along the way, without any real plans for it. But as a college student on Boston's South Shore in the early 1970s, I found a way to use it. A senior psychology major, I was required to carry out a year-long field placement; my fellow students were volunteering for kindergarten and nursing home assignments, but I felt the need for something more unique.

Having spent much of my youth writing earnest letters to the aging Helen Keller and reading about her teacher, Annie Sullivan, I was drawn to the possibility of designing a field placement at Annie's own school, Perkins School for the Blind, in Watertown, Massachusetts. Perkins and my college agreed, and I was assigned to assist in the after-school program in a house of boys who were deaf and blind.

There were half a dozen little fellows with varying degrees of hearing and vision loss in that house, but on my first visit, one child was missing.

Todd Patkus was in the hospital, undergoing surgery meant to improve the little vision he had. It was a risky procedure; doctors knew that if it wasn't successful, he would lose his sight altogether.

By the day of my second visit, eight-year-old Todd had returned to the house. The chart near the houseparents' office, identifying each child by vision status, had been hastily updated: "Todd Patkus—deaf, partially-sighted" had been crossed out and the word "blind" had been scrawled in pencil above his name.

"Toddy" and I became special friends that year. A supervisor assigned me to help Todd with his sudden disorientation, painful grief, and radically changed social and educational needs. Our two hearts touched, child and almost-adult, both groping to find our path, both yearning for independence when others felt we weren't quite ready for it, both longing just to be important to someone. Somehow, I recognized in Todd's unpredictable mix of joy, rage, curiosity, and frustration something of my own inner turmoil. We became friends.

My name, Rayelenn, although only eight letters long, is unusual, and many people seem to find it difficult to accept. The staff, fearing that it was too long for Todd to fingerspell, insisted he be allowed to call me Raye, a nickname I particularly disliked and had avoided all my life. But "Raye" it was.

The staff told me that between my visits, Todd would spell "Raye-Raye-Raye" and sign "Where is Raye?" repeatedly until I arrived. We were inseparable during my regular visits to Perkins. We learned Braille together, playing Scrabble and Go Fish to make a game out of recognizing the raised dots symbolizing letters of the alphabet and numbers. We learned to talk together, he leading the way in teaching me sign language, and the "tactile" method of signing where his hands, hovering gently over mine, learned to understand by feel the graceful words that previously he had experienced by limited vision.

We took walks around the beautiful Perkins campus, first hand in hand, then with his hand on my elbow, and later, as he became proficient with his child-sized white cane, with Todd careering joyfully around me, eager to lead me to his favorite places and show me his special treasures. We loved each other, the eager little fellow with the shaggy blonde hair, dimpled chin, sly childish wit, and bubbling good humor, and the earnest college senior looking for direction and purpose in life.

The spring arrived, the semester began to draw to a close, and senior comps and graduation were in the air. I submitted final journal entries to my supervising professor, wrote a research paper on sensory impairments, completed work for my other classes, and took my finals.

Dreading my last visit with Todd, I postponed it for as long as possible, waiting until nearly the last day of the semester. I knew it would be hard to say goodbye, to help him understand that my time with him was finished, that I had to move on to other commitments. In psychology classes, I had been coached on "closure issues," but I knew that despite such preparation, it would be a wrenching time for us both.

I rode the subway to Boston, boarded the old green trolley to Watertown, and hurried to Todd's group house, accompanied by the pealing of the bells in the Perkins School bell tower. When I arrived, he was not there. No one had remembered to call me to tell me that he had another commitment. He wouldn't be back for hours. I had to leave.

Soon after, I wrote him a letter, struggling with my little Braille stylus and slate, trying my best to punch the dots correctly so he could read it himself. I don't know if he ever received it. I never heard back. Perkins closed for the summer; I wasn't able to make contact.

I lost touch with the lovely little boy who had so opened my eyes to a new vision of the world and of love. I alternately imagined him grieving over my unexplained disappearance, or, more likely, forgetting as he grew up that I had ever existed.

I moved to Washington, D.C., for graduate study and eventually a position as instructor of English at Gallaudet University, the world's only university for deaf people. I became proficient in the language I had always yearned to embrace and qualified as a certified sign language interpreter.

Many years later, a decade and a half or more, during a break between classes, as I passed through the Gallaudet English department office, I unwittingly looked over the shoulder of a colleague typing on the office computer. "TODD PATKUS" the letter's address line read.

I trembled. "Terry, sorry—I, I couldn't help but see your monitor. Sorry. But—who's that you're writing to?"

"Student of mine. Todd Patkus. Bright, very bright. Capable. Well-read. Studies philosophy as a hobby, bless his heart. Reads and writes a couple of languages, quite knowledgeable in astronomy. But he's been cutting classes, and if he doesn't watch himself, he's going to flunk my course. No reason for it. Writing him a warning letter. Know him?"

"I think so. I used to. I mean, when he was a child. Is he blind? Deaf-blind?"

"Yeah, that's him. Coming for an appointment. Go out the main entrance; you can probably head him off and say hello."

Moments later, on the sidewalk, I squinted through my tears as I watched a tall, blond, shaggy-haired young man with a dimpled chin stride toward my building, white cane tapping confidently. I entertained a momentary image of the cartoon pictures children impress on Silly Putty and then stretch out wildly; the years had done nothing to change this boy but to stretch him from four feet to six. As he neared, I reached out and softly tapped his elbow. He abruptly stopped, signed "Who?" and lifted his hands, poising them to hover over mine as I answered.

"You probably don't remember me," I signed, his hands resting gently on mine. "I used to play with you after school at Perkins when you were a little boy."

His left hand swiftly clamped down on mine, arresting the flow of words. We stood frozen in the warm sunlight. He slowly raised his right hand and gracefully spelled: "R-A-Y-E." Gently, with the impish grin I remembered so well, he signed, "I've always remembered," and then he enfolded me in a crushing hug.

I've always remembered, too.

—RAYELENN SPARKS CASEY

Rayelenn Sparks Casey lives in Lancaster, Pennsylvania, with her husband, Stephen, an Episcopal priest, and their two young daughters, Emily Clare and Elizabeth Clare. Rayelenn is certified by The Registry of Interpreters for the Deaf and has been a professional sign language interpreter since 1979. Over the last 21 years she has interpreted for Desmond Tutu, the Dalai Lama, Sandra Day O'Connor, three Archbishops of Canterbury, the Chief Rabbi Of The United Kingdom, and countless deaf people in their daily life and work.

Contact Information

Abt, Christina
"Dream Dancer"
Crystal Hill Farm
9411 SandRock Road
Eden, NY 14057
E-mail: *christinaabt@
hotmail.com*

Berger, Stacy
"Just In the Nick of Time"
Biz Wiz Business Services,
Inc.
1145 Julia Heights Drive
Lantana, FL 33462
561-308-9641
561-586-7785
www.thebizwiz.cc
www.allaroundmom.com
E-mail: *thebizwiz
@hotmail.com*

Bergh, Ellen
"Restart Button"
PO Box 1072
Rosamond, CA 93560
661-256-1266
E-mail: *Mastermedia
@hughes.net*

Bowles-Reyer, Amy
"Blue Eyes"
Business phone: 301-652-
4302
*www.geocities.com/
amybowles/homepage.html*
E-mail: *amybowles@aol.com*

Casey, Rayelenn Sparks
"Never Forgotten"
429 Camp Meeting Road
Landisville, PA 17538
717-892-3080
E-mail: *Rayelenn@aol.com*

Donigian, Cindy A.
"A Gift for Daddy"
301 Hope Street
Washington, IL 61571

Ferris, Linda
"Out on a Ledge"
Lincoln Park, MI 48146
E-mail: *LAFRN10@aol.com*

Frost, Penny
"The Day My Heart Was
Kissed"
207-783-1998
E-mail: *frostfreelance
@yahoo.com*

Gibbs, Nancy B.
"What Can a Dime Say?,"
"A Dream Come True,"
"Moving Day" and "Golf
Course Romance"
P.O. Box 53
Cordele, GA 31010
E-mail: *DAISEYDOOD
@aol.com*

Gordon, Rose
"Tree Swing"
50511 Galaxy Drive
Granger, IN 46530
Phone/fax: 219-272-8090
E-mail: *On_Wings@att.net*

Haggerty, Deb
"The Spirit of Santa Claus"
PMB
#306, 2212 S Chickasaw
Trail
Orlando, FL 32825
E-mail: *deb@positiveconnect.
com*

Henley, Sue
"Jewel in My Crown"
1375 Bunker Hill Road
Cookeville, TN 38506
E-mail: *doupray2
@multipro.com*

Hodge, Marlisa
"Not Now, My Love"
8191-58th Way North
Pinellas Park, FL 33781
E-mail: *mhodge1
@tampabay.rr.com*

Housholder, Grace Witwer
"Tablecloth Stains"
816 Mott Street
Kendallville, IN 46755
219-347-0738
www.funnykids.com
E-mail: *tghous@noble.
cioe.com*

Iverson, Patti
"In Sickness and in
Sickness"
1224 North Modoc
Unit 24
Medford, OR 97504
E-mail: *randpi
@earthlink.net*

Jaffe, Azriela
"Mirror Image"
793 Sumter Drive
Yardley, PA 19067
215-321-5269
www.azriela.com
E-mail: *azriela
@mindspring.com*

January, Stefanie
"Favorite Song"
7538 Bloomington Avenue
South
Richfield, MN 55423
E-mail: *SJanuary1
@compuserve.com*

Jones, Pattie
"Haven of Comfort"
931 Wildwood Drive
Melbourne, FL 32940
321-242-6648
E-mail: *CHOOBAND
@aol.com*

Kiser, Roger Dean
"A Nickel's Worth" and
"Border Crossing"
100 Northridge Drive
Brunswick, GA 31525
912-261-0048 and
912-261-8300
E-mail: *trampolineone
@webtv.net*

Kisner, James A.
"The Treasured Box"
PO Box 38
Brunswick, OH 44212
E-mail: *PoppyK1@aol.com*

Kreuzer, Karen
"Safehaven"
435 Sixth Avenue
Pittsburgh, PA 15219
E-mail: *KKreuzer
@ReedSmith.com*

Krug, Amanda
"Dancing in the Aisles"
8883 Moll Drive
Fishers, IN 46038
317-845-8495
E-mail: *krug_family
@iquest.net*

Lay, Kathryn
"Falling in Love Again"
817-795-9413
E-mail: *rlay15@aol.com*

Lombard, Lynn
"Unlikely Friends" and
"A Sister's Love"
*www.heartwarmers4u.com/
members?lynn*
E-mail: *lynnlombard
@hotmail.com*

McMillion, Gloria S.
"First Date" and "Life Is a
Bucket Truck"
P.O. Box 62
Amelia, VA 23002
804-561-2045
E-mail: *gloriamcmillion
@amel.tds.net*

Merryfield, Lauren
"Love Far Beyond the
Physical"
19326 Bothell-Everett
Highway
sp15
Mill Creek, WA 98012
425-485-7916
*http://homestead.juno.com
/kabootle2/index.html*
E-mail: *kabootle2
@juno.com*

Norwood, Cheryl
"The Tarheel and the
Spitfire"
321 McLain Street
Canton, GA 30114
E-mail: *cnorwood
@ga.prestige.net*

Oliver, Jennifer
"Anthony's Wish"
Route 1
Box 562 Brenda Drive
Killeen, TX 76542

Reed, Jennifer B.
"Love at First Read" and
"Emotional Reunion"
www.weeonesmag.com
*http://home.quixnet.net/
~jreed*
E-mail: *jreed@quixnet.net*

Reuscher, Nancy
"Mid-Summer Night
Dreams"
WordSpirits
Sausalito, CA 94965
415-331-7218
nancy@wordspirits.com

Riccardi, Alison
"My Self-Esteem Lifter"
E-mail: *coca_cola_806
@yahoo.com*

Salzman, RoseMary
"Goodbye, My Love"
9920 State Road 22
Wild Rose, WI 54984
920-622-5202
E-mail: *prsalz@vbe.com*

Shepard, Glenda
"Their Song" and
"One Last Gift"
P.O. Box 1135
Havana, FL 32333
850-539-5264
912-762-3341
E-mail: *ROMEODUKE
OFWHIGHAM
@email.msn.com*

Stobbe, Joyce Carol
"Heaven-sent Blessing"
P.O. Box 2806
La Pine, OR 97739
541-536-1185
*www.heartwarmers4u.com/
members?sonjoy*
E-mail: *Jcjoy2u@aol.com*

Strauss, Jaime
"Love That Heals"
P.O. Box 7782 Gold Coast
Mail Center
SURFERS/Bundall,
Q4217 Australia
E-mail: *jaime
@joynet.com.au*

Stroupe, Nanci L.
"Friends for 43 Years"
123 Tide Mill Lane #41B
Hampton, VA 23669
E-mail: *ONENONI
@aol.com*

**Winter-Hartley,
Cindy M.**
"My Mother's Magic
Sandwich"
100 Cove Creek Drive
Apex, NC 27502
919-387-9951
E-mail:
cinwinhar@aol.com

Wooldridge, Connie D.
"Marriage Made in
Heaven"
PO Box 637
Winfield, KS 67156
316-221-9033
E-mail: *cwooldri@hit.net*